D0676791

JED HARRIS

A DANCE ON THE HIGH WIRE

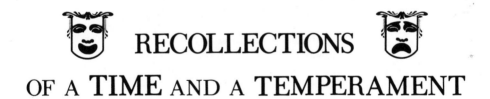 RECOLLECTIONS OF A TIME AND A TEMPERAMENT

CROWN PUBLISHERS, INC. NEW YORK

©1979 by Jed Harris

All rights reserved. No part of this book may be reproduced or utilized
in any form or by any means, electronic or mechanical, including
photocopying, recording, or by any information storage and retrieval
system, without permission in writing from the publisher.
Inquiries should be addressed to Crown Publishers, Inc.,
One Park Avenue, New York, N.Y. 10016

Printed in the United States of America

Published simultaneously in Canada by
General Publishing Company Limited

Library of Congress Cataloging in Publication Data
Harris, Jed.
A dance on the high wire.

1. Harris, Jed.   2.   Theatrical producers and
directors—United States—Biography.   I.   Title.
PN2287.H249A26   792'.0232'0924   [B]   79-15360
ISBN 0-517-53921-7

This book is for my old friend, Jacques Traubee

❧ A PROLOGUE OF SORTS: ❧
DEBUT

I SUPPOSE I CAN CLAIM WITH LORD BYRON THAT I AWOKE one morning to find myself famous. I had gone to bed at seven thirty of a cool September evening in 1926, exactly one hour before the curtain was to rise on the opening night's performance of *Broadway*. My telephone rang shortly after eleven o'clock, and I heard my press agent, S. N. Behrman, report that the play was a colossal success.

"The house lights have been up for almost a minute," he said, "and they're still applauding the show. I've never seen anything like it."

"Where are you talking from?"

"I'm in the box office. Can't you hear them?"

"Yes, I think so."

"It's come off exactly as you predicted. Well, Jed, you are going to be enormously rich. You will have a splendid country house and entertain the great of the world."

"The great of this world are all in the next world, Sam," I said. "Right now I'm still famished for sleep."

"Better take your receiver off the hook, or you won't get any sleep at all. Good-night."

My absence from the Broadhurst Theatre on that reputedly momentous occasion would soon provide the first frail under-pinnings to my "legendary" reputation. In a matter of hours a Broadway columnist would call me to confirm the rumor that I had spent the evening at home asleep.... "With so much at stake, how could you possibly have done a thing like that?" he said. "It was really quite simple," I replied. "I took off my clothes, got into bed, and closed my eyes." He subsequently described me as enigmatic.

I might have told him that for me the adventure of producing *Broadway* was finished in Hartford the night before the New York opening. I had been obsessed day and night for six months with that production. As the curtain fell on the last out-of-town performance, I was dead certain that it would be a great success. At that moment I succumbed to a fit of exhaustion and, somewhat to my surprise, discovered that I had no desire to see it ever again.

I might also have told him that at the age of twenty-one, as a reporter for a theatrical trade paper, I had suffered through a whole season of opening nights. The commercial theatre at the time was little more than mass entertainment, barely above the level of the imbecilities on the television screens today. Except for Eugene O'Neill, whose *Anna Christie* had reached Broadway, the other "modern" playwrights, Robert E. Sherwood, George S. Kaufman and Marc Connelly, Ben Hecht and Charles MacArthur, Maxwell Anderson, Philip Barry and Sidney Howard, were still incubating somewhere off in the wings.

Hardly out of my teens, I had already come to the conclusion that I could direct and produce plays far better than anyone on Broadway, an opinion I was prudent enough to keep to myself. And I found the atmosphere of show business increasingly trivial and childish. This growing mood was intensified one night when I had dinner with a fellow reporter. He had found a charming apartment in Queens, he said, and was about to marry the girl of his dreams and settle down to cozy married life. His eyes glowed with the joy of that prospect. He could not possibly have imagined how this news depressed me.

I suddenly caught a glimpse of the possibility of getting involved myself with a girl and marrying and facing a life sentence of domestic bliss—and acute professional boredom. And my passion for the theatre was all but stifled by the junk that I saw on Broadway. I soon found myself dreading those opening nights, with their claques of actors' friends, producer's friends, and author's friends, all clapping like trained seals at every stage entrance and exit, more often than not in the face of what was only too obviously going to be a disastrous evening.

A DANCE ON THE HIGH WIRE

After that dinner with my friend, I went home, wrote my boss a note of resignation, and went off the next day, like Chicken Little, to see the world. I was gone for the better part of two years.

In that time I explored most of the Eastern Shore of Maryland, I was the pampered guest for five days of the fire department in Greensburg, Pennsylvania, I served briefly as a Latin tutor for a feebleminded youth in Peru, Indiana (now famous as the birthplace of Cole Porter and the confection of the best fudge in the world),* I spent a week on an Indian reservation, and acquired a lifelong hostility to the government of the United States of America. But most of the time I was merely a tramp, and as such I was given free lodging in nine jails all the way from Suffolk, Virginia, where I was arrested as a possible deserter from the Navy and spent a long night in the company of three despondent black boys, to Missouri Valley, Iowa, where anybody with a good flashlight might have found me late one night sitting on a cold cement floor in a windowless dungeonlike brick hut, since the only available cot, an affair of iron latticework covered with dirty old newspapers, was unfortunately occupied. But whatever the discomforts, it never once occurred to me that I might have been better off attending opening nights on Broadway.

Not surprisingly, the columnist asked none of the questions that a good journalist might have put to me. On the whole it was probably better that way. It is after all not too difficult to be enigmatic; all you really have to do is look down the end of your nose and say nothing.

In the half century since it was first produced, I have heard literally hundreds of people say that *Broadway* was the best show they had ever seen. I think I can now at this late date say the same thing. "I cannot for the life of me think of the man or woman who would not be deeply absorbed by *Broadway*," wrote Alexander Woollcott in one of the very few of his theatre opinions in which I could concur. If the show

---

* And a droll but oddly fitting counterpart to Lübeck, Germany, once the home town of J. S. Bach and the still acknowledged world capital of marzipan.

captivated Alphonse Capone, it was also received with the same enthusiasm by the Prince of Wales. On the opening night of the London production, Bernard Shaw, H. G. Wells, Arnold Bennett, J. M. Barrie, and Siegfried Sassoon stood with the rest of that first-night audience and applauded the company for a good five minutes after the final curtain.

In 1937, in the Grill Room of the Savoy Hotel in London, when Adele Astaire introduced me to Winston Churchill, she reminded him that I was the producer of *Broadway*. The old boy, then scraping the bottom of his political career, was seated behind a brandy bottle at his famed round table in the bow window of the room, with an enormous cigar in his hand, surrounded by theatre people, among whom I recognized the dancer Tilly Losch and Rudolph Kommer, Reinhardt's business agent. "Ah, *Broadway*," he said. "That was one of the really great theatrical experiences of my life."

Set in the back room of a second-rate nightclub, a sort of traffic center for chorus girls scampering to their dressing rooms to change their costumes during the cabaret show, it was also the unofficial meeting place for bootleggers and gunmen. Thus *Broadway* marked the first appearance on the American stage of members of organized crime. Scenes of violence alternated with bursts of comedy, while dance music was being played in the club offstage between shows. Murder, irony, humor—all these were mingled in such a crafty fashion that the effect was simply spellbinding.

Its success in New York was matched by its success in London, Paris, Berlin, and Rome. It was even a hit in Moscow, where the communist authorities, characteristically light-fingered, simply pinched the rights and produced it without bothering to pay for them, exactly as they would later do with *The Front Page*.

On tour *Broadway* broke all attendance records everywhere. In Detroit, for example, it played to capacity business for almost six months. Commercially it was of course a bonanza, and the money came rolling in like a tidal wave. In less than two weeks the entire cost of the production of *Broadway* ($13,000) had been recovered. And my bank account, hitherto a Cassiuslike affair, began to swell out into the more benign proportions of Mr. Pickwick. I calculated, quite accurately, that my share of the profits would come to three quarters of a million dollars, a sum with the purchasing power of more than $5 million today.

The money, whatever it amounted to—and it soon amounted to a great deal—was something outside my life. I continued to live in a small apartment on West Tenth Street on the same scale as before, on about seventy-five dollars a week. The real importance of the money, apart from the help I could give my family, lay in the independence it gave me to do any play I liked without being compelled to go to others for backing. I had absolutely no desire for the things money could buy. Indeed, I had a horror of possessions. The only things I accumulated from time to time were books, but I gave hundreds of them away. I had traveled light, a *voyageur sans bagage*, all my life.

Months after the opening of *Broadway*, when my bank balance must have risen to over fifty thousand dollars, I noticed a fawn-colored topcoat in a shopwindow on Fifth Avenue and found myself wishing I could have one like that. I must have walked another six blocks before it occurred to me that I could now afford to buy a hundred of them. But then, I thought, I already own a topcoat. What would I do with two of them?

Money is a little like love. Anything one might be tempted to say about it has already been said before. And it is a field traditionally rampant with misquotation. One frequently hears of John Maynard Keynes's remark to Lytton Strachey that "it is impossible to exaggerate the importance of money." Now if that were attributed to Henry Luce, one might yawn and turn to the pages of *Newsweek*. I find it difficult to imagine anyone as brilliant and perceptive as Lord Keynes saying anything so utterly banal and questionable. I choose to believe that what Keynes really said is that it is impossible to exaggerate the *respect* for money.

This was a lesson I was now discovering for myself. I frequently found myself trapped between embarrassment and laughter as people with whom I had always exchanged casual hellos now addressed me with almost absurd deference. Even the members of my staff spoke to me in awed tones. Everybody seemed to be affected by the money while I was still a bit self-conscious about paying for railway tickets. I had traveled all over the country absolutely free of charge on the fastest, most luxurious trains in the West. It is true that I usually sat on the tender, always careful to stay out of sight of the fireman and engineer. But on a hot summer night when I was sitting with perhaps half-a-dozen fellow travelers enjoying the breeze under a brilliant prairie moon, an I.W.W. organizer, sprawled out beside me, took his pipe out of his mouth and said, "It would take a son of a bitch with a heart of stone not to feel sorry for those poor, suffering, rich bastards sweating in their upholstered bunks underneath us." (All this was of course in the days before air-conditioning.)

If the "great of the world" did not immediately come knocking at my door, my sudden elevation brought me to the attention of some of the most distinguished real-estate brokers in the country. In rapid succession I was offered a plantation in South Carolina—not too far, I was assured, from Hobcaw Colony, the baronial estate of Bernard Baruch—a five-thousand-acre ranch, fully stocked, in Wyoming, and a luxurious spread in New Hampshire with a private lake and a whole mountain I could call my own. However, I must admit there was no offer of a shooting box in Scotland.

And there was a small stream of ladies, the kind referred to in the Hearst press as society women, who arrived, one by one, elegant and fragrant, to proclaim their undying devotion to the theatre. Their lives, it appeared, were being tragically wasted on bridge, dinner parties, and stuffy charity affairs, because they simply had nothing else to *do*. Subjecting me to a scrutiny worthier of a more ornamental object, they announced, each one in turn, that they were prepared, without salary of course, to do anything for an opportunity to serve the sacred muse of the drama. *Anything.* It took me a little while to realize that I was, in the eloquent gutter language of Broadway, nothing more than fresh meat.

And there was a rather broader stream of callers, most of them unknown to me, who came to congratulate me on my

6   A DANCE ON THE HIGH WIRE

good fortune. These identified themselves as relatives of mine or, at least, relatives *of* relatives. And by what was probably pure coincidence, they all needed money. Rather than spend my time probing their consanguinity, I chose the path of accommodation.

I was also invited to countless dinner parties, almost entirely by people I had never met. I responded to few and accepted none. This of course marked me as odd. And when people heard that I usually ate at the Automat on Broadway, I was put down as even odder. I was of course much too busy to give these matters any thought at all.

But when I turned down an offer of a party to be given for me at Walter Wanger's house so that I could meet some "important" people, Wanger was upset. And *that* did matter to me. He had generously befriended me at a time when I was in a most difficult situation.

What had happened was that in February of 1926, just a bit more than six months before the opening of *Broadway*, I had produced a comedy by the poet John V. A. Weaver and George Abbott called *Love 'Em and Leave 'Em*. The opening night went well enough to assure me of at least a moderately successful run. And the occasion was made more festive by the gentle descent of a few large, feathery snowflakes as the audience was leaving the theatre.

But things were not so festive in the morning. That light, lovely snowfall of the night before had turned into a full blizzard. The city lay under a blanket of snow four feet deep and more. Subway traffic was almost at a standstill, the Long Island Railroad had been forced to suspend operations, and there were no taxis in the streets. Indeed, the newspapers were comparing the disaster to the Great Blizzard of 1888. By one o'clock that afternoon, despite quite good reviews, not a single person had come to the box office of the theatre. The bleak prospect was that we would be forced to play to empty houses for the next few nights. What was even more bleak was the probability that I would not be able to meet my payroll on Saturday.

On a desperate chance, I called the office of Walter

Wanger, then a newly installed vice-president at Paramount, to ask for an appointment. After some delay his secretary reported that he could see me at four fifty that afternoon. That would give me ten minutes to ask him if his company was sufficiently interested in the film rights of the play to guarantee a bank loan I might be forced to make to see me through the week. All I knew about Wanger was that he was young, rich, and, what made him a rare find in the picture business of that era, a college graduate. And that he was married to a fabulously beautiful ex-chorus girl named Justine Johnson.

It took me almost twenty-five minutes to make my way through the heavy snowdrifts between Times Square and the Paramount offices, then on Fifth Avenue and Forty-second Street. I got there exactly on time and was immediately overwhelmed by my first glimpse of a movie executive's office, which struck me as almost oriental in splendor. And a perfect background for Wanger who, with his dark handsome features, looked like a young Persian prince. (I cannot help thinking how much that image might have pleased him. On the other hand, if I said he looked like a Jewish prince, I don't think he would have been pleased at all. A few years later when we had become really good friends, I was amused to find him almost proud of his ignorance of Jewish history and Jewish life in general. He had been born in San Francisco into a very well-to-do German-Jewish family, the darling of his mother and two adoring aunts. So anxious were these devoted ladies to shield him from the hazards of Jewishness that they decided to preserve him in the state in which he was born, pure and uncircumcised. Sadly enough, this turned out to be a mistake. At the age of forty, as a result of various pains and discomforts, and some indignities of which he did not care to speak, he was literally forced to endure the long-deferred humiliation of circumcision. But by that time, fortunately, those adoring ladies were dead.)

Wanger seemed surprisingly impressed by my status as a "Yale man." I hastened to assure him that I was nothing of the sort, that I had merely lived in a dormitory at Yale and read some books there, without any feeling for the place beyond acute boredom. And I was so worried about the time that was being wasted on so pointless a matter that I interrupted the course of conversation and stated my problem. Like a true prince he waved my concerns aside. He made no effort to conceal the pleasure he had derived from the play and particularly from the production. And he offered to call the bank and help arrange any loan I might need.

For me the interview was now over. I was suddenly aware that I was tired and that I had had nothing more than a cup of coffee for lunch. And my legs were cold and wet from the snow I had waded through. But if the meeting seemed over for me, for Wanger it had not quite begun. I sat there for the next three hours answering dozens of questions. By the time the meeting was over at eight fifteen that evening, we had explored the whole range of modern literature and drama, English, French, German, and Russian. And then we began to talk about films, and Wanger was astonished to find that I could describe films like Von Stroheim's *Greed* and Charles Chaplin's *A Woman of Paris* not merely in exact sequence but almost shot for shot. Before we parted, Wanger asked for my home phone number. The next morning he called to invite me to lunch with Adolph Zukor and Jesse Lasky in their private dining room.

A Hungarian immigrant, Zukor had started out as a small businessman while Lasky had spent his youth blowing a trumpet in a musical act in vaudeville. Now they were the chief officers and the largest stockholders in the greatest motion-picture company in the world. The value of their shares would rise through the next three years to the level of colossal personal fortunes. And then, following the stock-market crash, they would find themselves teetering on the edge of bankruptcy. Indeed Lasky was destroyed as a factor in the business.

But the day I was introduced to them they were almost at the zenith of their careers: Lasky, tall, blue-eyed, and genial, was not nearly so impressive as Adolph Zukor, who was small and compact, and whose shrewd gray eyes suggested hidden reservoirs of subtlety and strength. (Zukor was the sole survivor of that period* and at the age of one hundred was still the honorary chairman of the board of Paramount.)

Lasky began by saying that he had never heard Wanger speak of anyone as glowingly as he had spoken of me. (Later I would recognize myself as only one of Wanger's sudden enthusiasms. In time they would include the English economist Barbara Ward, whom he once described as the most intelligent woman in the world, and colonic irrigation, which he saw as a cure-all for practically everything that ails troubled mankind.)

Zukor said little during these preliminary remarks. Then, rather casually, he said, "We are prepared to offer you a contract for three years at $50,000, $75,000, and $100,000 a year."

I had been wondering what he was going to offer me for the film rights to *Love 'Em and Leave 'Em*. Now I drew a deep breath and said, "Nobody ever paid me more than $150 a week." Everybody laughed. I knew precisely what Cinderella felt when she stood up for the first time in her glass slippers.

"I would certainly love to lay my hands on all that money," I said, "if only I didn't have to sign a contract and become an employee of a corporation."

"All of us here are employees of a corporation," said Zukor. "And we don't find it so bad. What is it you have against corporations?"

"The thing I have against corporations is that they are corporations. That means large bodies of men dedicated to making profits for stockholders in order to hold on to their jobs. And to do that they must seek for accommodation among themselves—that is, they must cooperate. And if there is one word in the English language I hate, it's the word *cooperation*."

"I think it is a wonderful word," said Zukor. "How could the important things in the world be accomplished without cooperation?"

---

* Still true when this was written a couple of years ago.

"I am sorry to disagree with you, Mr. Zukor. The greatest things have been accomplished not only without cooperation but against overwhelming opposition. Anyway, my experience is that cooperation always requires me to do something I don't want to do, or, what is even worse, not to do something I want very much to do. I'm just too much of a maverick for anything like that. The first time I found myself balked by some decent, kindly executive on the ground that Paramount is a publicly owned company and that what I wanted to do, however lovely and noble it might appear to be, would not be in the interest of the stockholders, I wouldn't even bother to reply. I would just reach for my hat and leave the company flat. And I have no doubt your board would be so glad to see me go that they'd throw me a banquet and a free trip to Europe."

"Suppose we were to let you choose a story for your first picture, what would it be?" said Lasky.

"Dreiser's *An American Tragedy.*"

"Why pick out a tragedy?" said Zukor. "Isn't there enough tragedy in life? Why should we add to it?"

"Ah, you see, Mr. Zukor, if I had signed that contract only a few minutes ago, I would already be dictating my resignation. In the first place, the story is not a tragedy. For a first-rate novelist, Dreiser writes very badly. There are times when I suspect he doesn't even understand the English language. There is nothing tragic about the hero of the story. He is merely a clumsy, rather squalid young man who might have gotten away with murder and lived out his life as a rich, respected citizen. It was simply his hard luck to get caught. The essence of the story lies in the suspense of the big situation: will he get away with it? In the actual case which took place upstate some years ago and which Dreiser very faithfully copied, Chester Gillette, which was of course the real name of Clyde Griffith, looked as though he might beat the case and go free. But because he has no dramatic sense, Dreiser left out the best scene in the actual story. Gillette had stood up very well in cross-examination. Then, suddenly, the prosecutor introduced the suitcase the boy had brought along on his camping trip with his pregnant girl. From that suitcase he produced a brand-new pair of white flannel trousers. 'Did you intend to rough it in the woods in these trousers?' he asked. Next he took out a new tennis racket and then he produced a paper box out of the bag, opened it, and extracted a brand-new tennis ball. Now he strolled around the courtroom, deliberately bouncing the ball on the floor. The horror in the boy's eyes confirmed what everyone in the courtroom knew: the repeated thud of that bouncing ball would send him bouncing into the electric chair."

Zukor's eyes were blazing. "My God," he said. "I must say that's a wonderful scene."

Naturally Wanger was very much disappointed by my rejection of Zukor's offer.

"I can't help admiring the guts of anybody as broke as you are turning down an offer like that," he said. "But I think you have made a great mistake. Do you know something? In ten years you and I might be running Paramount."

I laughed. "I haven't the faintest interest in the world in running Paramount. The only running I know anything about is running away. In going to Yale I was really running away from home. Then I ran away from Yale. And after running around Paris and London, I got a job on Broadway and ran away from that. And there is so much I detest about show business that one of these days I suppose I'll start running again."

(Paramount did buy the film rights to *An American Tragedy*, and the press attributed the purchase of the rights to the interest I had created for it.)

Now I felt obliged once more to let down my good friend Wanger. I explained as patiently as I could that I was committed to producing three new plays within the year, that I was planning a production of *Broadway* in London as well as casting five touring companies, that of the three new plays I was preparing, two had to be completely rewritten, and one was only half finished, that each of these ventures presented awesome problems in casting, and that my average day's work lasted fifteen hours, and that I sometimes slept around the clock on Sundays to conserve my strength.

"I have no time to meet people," I said, "no matter how

'important' they may be. Anyway, so-called important people are likely to be rich people, and I just don't like rich people."

Wanger thought for a moment. "Maybe it would be a good idea for you to go to Vienna and have Dr. Freud probe your psyche for the cause of such an irrational attitude," he said.

"I don't need anybody poking around in my past for the origin of my prejudices against the rich. I got them legitimately in New Haven, Connecticut, and it's probably the most important part of my education at Yale."

Oddly enough, I had loved Yale, and between the ages of ten and twelve, I enjoyed the place immensely. I was not, like the late Norbert Weiner, a prodigy. Nor was that Yale the venerable institution, so admirably operated by the Yale Corporation, across the road from the Taft Hotel bar in New Haven. It was another Yale, a boy's paradise, invented by a marvelously fertile hack writer pen-named Burt L. Standish, Jr., who turned out the Merriwell stories by the hundreds. No doubt these stories owed something of their innocence to a telling advantage of the author's. He had never laid eyes on the real place.

The real Yale, as even a retarded worldling like myself was aware, was bound to be different. But I found that difference too chilling to face. So I retreated to the shelter of my old secret fantasies, as older men, bruised by the world, cling to the small pieties of a religion they no longer believe in. I was obviously unprepared to enter the real world.

But there was another world waiting for schlemiels like me, and in that world I thankfully lost myself. Like a man with a small but rapidly growing business, rushing to the bank for more and more money, I became a frenzied borrower. But my bank was only the old Linonian Library. There I discovered the world of books. I did not read books—I devoured them. Like a lover I fell asleep with them in my arms and awoke enveloped in them. I soon became a creature of the spirit world, subsisting on air and water, and fobbing off my baser nature with false promises and an occasional ham sandwich.

I recently encountered a startling portrait of myself during that period. It was in a passage, the work of an unnamed writer, quoted in an article by Alfred Kazin, in which the author describes a boy studying the Torah:

> He has roamed as far and as wide as an ancient who has outlived the years of Methuselah! He has been in Mesopotamia, in Canaan, in Egypt, in Persia and Medea, in Susa, its capital, and in multiple other lands as far as India and Cathay; also the wilderness and the desert he has frequented, and there he has hearkened to many marvelous things ... of a sort which to all other people are an incomprehensible mystery; but among Jews it is a common everyday event. Only with Jewish children does it transpire that they sit day and night rooted to one spot, not knowing what is happening round abouts, what they need learn in order to live among people. . . . All thoughts are in another world, in other epochs; they are oblivious to the world right under their noses and devote themselves entirely to that which transpired long ago, for which eyes and other crude human senses are not so much needed as an acute imaginative faculty—a stark naked soul—devoid of a body, almost devoid of life itself ... he is not exactly a native, but resides somewhere over there. . . . His times are beforetimes, his world is another. . . .

My competence as a guide in Mesopotamia might have been debatable. But in time I got to know my way around the London of Shakespeare and Marlowe, and of Fielding and Thackeray, the St. Petersburg and Moscow of Dostoevski and Tolstoi, the Paris of Balzac and Huysmans, even the Rome of Juvenal and Plautus. At least now I was a schlemiel who had read some books. But Yale remained alien ground. It was as if a wall had risen between us.

One beautiful morning that wall unceremoniously collapsed, and with something of a crash, I entered the real world. I was staring at a line in a poem in one of the college magazines: "When Jews and other scum beyond human ken make Yale fraternities . . ." I had been sitting in my pajamas in a chair, the open copy of the magazine in my lap. And then I heard someone say, "What's the matter? Are you ill?"

The voice was that of Elliott Cohen, a senior. I was fully dressed and had apparently crossed the campus.

A DANCE ON THE HIGH WIRE

"Did you see that thing in the *Record*?" I said.

"What thing?"

I repeated the line.

"Oh, that," said Cohen indifferently. "What about it?"

"I'm going to shoot the son of a bitch who wrote that," I said.

"Really? Have you got a gun?" he asked politely.

"I think I know where I can get one."

"Well, now," said Cohen. "I hope you won't mind if I ask you as a favor to forget that you mentioned the matter to me. Now there's a whole lot of different things in the world I'd like to be. But not an accessory."

"All right." I had started to move away when Cohen grabbed my arm.

"By the way," he said, "I guess it's just a sheer act of Providence but there happens to be a jug of half-hard cider on the windowsill up in my room. And I think maybe you'd better help me break into it. Then you can go on about your business. You understand, of course, that business's gotta be a total mystery to me."

"I remember quite clearly. You don't want to be an accessory."

Cohen was a rather languid, disdainful refugee from Mobile, Alabama, with a large, knowing, childlike face and extremely casual manners. He was the first Southerner I had ever known, and I was enchanted by the way he talked. When at times his Southern accent seemed to drop away, I could always make him laugh by saying, "Talk nigra to me, boy." What we shared in common was a love of ballplayers and vaudeville comedians. But he had impressed me from the moment I met him. I had merely asked him if he would come along to the gymnasium with me.

"What for?" he said suspiciously, as if I had proposed something shady. "You mean you want me to go and develop mah muscles?"

"Why not?"

This attitude was a revelation to me. As far as I knew, the value of muscular development had never been questioned by anyone before.

"Now, these muscles you're talkin' about—what am I gonna

do with 'em after they git developed? Jes' stand around waitin' for 'em to turn to fat?"

I was a bit shaken as we walked up the stairs to Cohen's room in Vanderbilt Hall. A sense of personal disaster had taken hold of me. I had no memory of dressing or leaving my dormitory. I knew a man who might have lent me a gun but I had no recollection of any plan to get in touch with him. I had reacted to this business like a very young fish, suddenly stunned by an underwater explosion. This discovery of my vulnerability was a bitter dose to swallow. Losing status is always something of a wrench, even the status of a schlemiel, and for the first time in my life, I badly wanted a drink.

But now my luck took a turn for the better. The cider proved to be a little more than half hard. For a while we drank in silence—that is, Cohen sipped but I really drank.

"Well, now," said Cohen, "it seems to me that if you gonna shoot this yere fellah, you also gotta shoot the editors of the magazine for printin' that piece. After all, the guy you want to shoot only wrote it. Now, if you also shoot all the editors, then as a matter of common justice, there must be some members of the faculty you gotta shoot too, because some of them aroun' here are not merely tolerant of such views, but support them."

I could not deny this so I held out my empty glass.

"Now," said Cohen, as he poured fresh drinks, "that brings up the economic factor. Are you flush?"

"No."

"Then where the hell are you gonna get the money to buy all that ammunition?"

"I hadn't thought about it."

"You hadn't? Do you realize how many people you'll have to shoot aroun' here? Once you start in, you can't go playin' favorites, shootin' one guy here and then skippin' another guy over there. A shortage of bullets is going to make a mighty poor excuse. And you can't go pleadin' poverty in a matter of this kind. One way or anothuh you gotta be fair and shoot 'em all."

There is a lot of cider in a jug, so I filled my glass again.

"I was taught to believe that the aim of education was to

civilize men. Well, there isn't a goddamn thing about this place that has the remotest connection with civilization. Imagine spending a whole semester on rhetorical horseshit like Carlyle's *Heroes and Hero Worship*." I think by this time I was bellowing a little.

"My God," murmured Cohen. "You are not only a freshman in this college, but you're one of those total freshmen, born to spend your life pissing into the wind."

"All right, so I'm naive. But it's your duty as a senior to put me wise to a few things. Why the hell in this day and age would they insist that we go to chapel every morning?"

"You remember ol' pathetic fallacy?" said Cohen.

"Please don't talk about it. It always makes me sad."

"You oughta be sad. You have deliberately mistaken this place for an institution of learning. Whereas and whereas in plain fact it's a resort."

"They tell me chapel isn't compulsory in Bar Harbor. Why the hell do they make us go to church here?"

"Obviously in the hope that in time you may become a Christian gentleman, say like Otto Kahn.* And then you'll be able to spend *your* summers in Bar Harbor and skip chapel for the rest of your life."

I shook my head. "A very fat old pederast," I said, "asked a passing cockney boy to pick up the spectacle case he had dropped on the sidewalk. 'I beg your pardon?' said the boy. 'I said will you please bend down and pick up my spectacle case?' The boy took a good look at the old fellow and said, 'Not bloody likely.'"

"Damn it," said Cohen, as he stared at the empty jug, "this cider set me back thirty-five cents."

By the time Cohen killed himself a few years ago, he was the highly respected editor of the magazine *Commentary*. But even as an undergraduate, he was a civilizing force.

If my attendance in classes had until now been irregular, it was henceforth to become exceedingly rare. As for Battel

* One of the great patrons of the Metropolitan Opera, a senior partner in Kuhn, Loeb and Company, was a Christian convert who died an Episcopalian.

Chapel, I never saw the inside of it again. By the middle of my sophomore year, my connection with the college curriculum had grown so tenuous that I had to ask a friend whether I had signed up for chemistry or geology at the beginning of the term. Examinations lay directly ahead, and I had of course never shown up at either class.

"Geology," he said.

"How can you remember that?"

"You said you had a bad experience with chlorine gas in high school."

"Ah, yes." I had taken a whiff of something yellow in a test tube and fallen flat on my back. "Well, I'd bet my life against a dime that there's nobody on earth who knows less about geology than I do."

"Such odds are foolish."

"They're for suckers. Don't you see that? This is a sure thing, Roger."

"Nothing is sure."

I was in something of a quandary as I left this cautious fellow, the son of a small-town banker. I had just come from breakfast on Elm Street, and I was not at all sure I wanted to walk back a hundred yards or so to the co-op and blow twenty cents on a couple of old geology examination papers. Twenty cents was a lot of money, and besides, I was much closer to the old Linonian where there was a whole stack of books waiting to be picked up. As my academic standing declined, my status at the library had soared. And I was now permitted to take out as many books as I liked.

But at the moment, my total ignorance of geology was critical. Not that a failure to pass the course would have bothered me. But it might well call attention to my wholesale truancies and lead to my expulsion. I was already under suspension for cutting chapel. But this was only a minor matter. (When the letter of expulsion finally came, I simply ignored it.) What was really at stake was my vanity as the author of the Ape Theory of Passing Grades at Yale. Marks at the time were on a scale of 0 to 400, but it took only 200 to pass. Thus Yale was perhaps the one place on earth where you could be safe by being only half safe.

According to the Ape Theory, any normal, reasonably healthy baboon could achieve passing grades in any arts course at Yale, but a trained chimpanzee would graduate with honors. This doctrine had won me some small notice, but it did not go unchallenged. A graduate student in zoology wrote me a letter deploring my ignorance of primates. He even took the trouble to draw up a list of eminent baboons. Among these he named fifteen United States Senators, five German theologians, nine faculty wives, and the entire student body of the Sheffield Scientific School. (Ironically enough, the zoologist, later a distinguished curator, was himself bitten a few years ago by a female baboon. The newspaper account I read unfortunately gave no indication of the nature of their relations.)

As I walked across the campus on my way to the co-op, the clock in the church tower struck ten. On an impulse I wandered into a class in American history and took a back seat. It was a class I seldom visited. In the college Baedecker it was rated as something that need not detain the tourist. But it was nevertheless a rather restful place to drop into. The professor who was in charge smiled a good deal and showed extraordinarily large teeth, and he was unfailingly polite. But what really fascinated me was the rear view of a large creature in the front row. The back of his neck rose in a dead straight line to the top of his head, which was pink and yellow. It looked like the work of an indigent carver who had to make do with a block of wood not quite large enough for his purpose—a hard wood, probably teak, I thought, judging by its color and other things. Affixed to each side of the block was a tiny pale pink shell, which I chose to attribute to a whim of the artist's fanciful little daughter.

It was the proprietor of this head who was now being addressed by the professor. "Tell us, if you please," he said, "what was the Dred Scott Decision?"

There was a long pause. The head remained immobile. Behind his spectacles, the professor's eyes gleamed encouragingly and his half-opened mouth exposed a considerable number of the teeth previously mentioned. What great decisions, I couldn't help wondering, must be rolling around in the dense, fibrous, constricted quarters of that block, what memories of John Marshall . . . Taney . . . perhaps even of Coke . . . ?

"Would you be kind enough to repeat that, sir?"

I marveled. The first time I had heard that question was in the seventh grade in Monmouth Street School in Newark, New Jersey. But there was a dramatic tension in the air of Miss Susan Van Steamburgh's classroom. A love of American history was her dominating passion. And to fail to give the correct answer to one of her questions and be forced to face the contempt in those stormy, blue, Dutch pirate's eyes of hers was enough to make you wish you had cut your throat before the school bell rang. The afternoon she read us the Bill of Rights, hammering out the words with the art of an old-fashioned classical actress, left us in a state of delirium.

The star of that class was a fiercely patriotic, immigrant Slav girl named Katrina, a shy, sturdy child, staring myopically out of very pale eyes and still troubled by a foreign accent. But in the history class she was Saint Joan, Edith Cavell, and Molly Pitcher all rolled into one. And a worthy histrionic match for her teacher.

"And what, Katrina, was the American reply to this despicable French proposal?" said Miss Van Steamburgh one day. Her tone was scathing.

"Milly-ons for de-fance," cried Katrina, "but not one panny for tribune!" On these last words her voice rose to a defiant shriek that almost brought us out of our seats. And the next day we all brought bits of money to buy glasses for Katrina.

How far I had come from the tension-ridden atmosphere of those days, I reflected, as the professor, carefully emphasizing each word, repeated the question.

"The Dred Scott Decision," the teak-head began firmly, as if the repetition of the question had cleared up some small hazy area in his mind, "was a decision"—here an unexpected querying note appeared as though he was anxious not to intrude on forbidden ground—"a decision involving a slave, an—uh—Negro slave whose name, I believe, was Dred Scott?"

"Ah, yes, quite right," murmured the professor approvingly. "And now if you please, will you tell us *what* that

A DANCE ON THE HIGH WIRE

decision *was?*" He sounded like an Alpine guide urging an exhausted climber up the last few meters to the top of the Matterhorn.

"That is the part, sir, that I don't quite seem to remember."

I noted with pleasure that of the ten questions in the geology examinations of the two previous years, nine and a half were identical. And the index of the official textbook I borrowed from the library was sheer perfection. It was the work of barely two hours to find and copy answers to the ten and a half questions. What a neat, dear, wholesome little science geology is, I thought, yielding up its secrets so sweetly.

The next day I carefully copied what I had written the day before. And early the next morning, before going to the examination hall, I copied the whole thing again. But that was hardly necessary. The answers simply flowed out of my pen of their own accord.

A glance at the questions in the examination confirmed my secret fear that I might be forced to hand in an absolutely perfect paper. This worried me. It was bad enough to be reproducing the exact language of the textbook. For the sake of verisimilitude as well as for my protective obscurity, I was anxious to make a few mistakes. The difficulty was that I did not know enough geology to make a decent, credible mistake. For the moment I even forgot that I did not know any geology at all. I reluctantly dismissed the matter as a minor though singularly tempting artistic problem.

Meanwhile my pen, utterly independent of these uneasy speculations, was racing shuttlewise across the page. I was spellbound watching it form letters, then words and sentences studded with terms like *igneous, sedimentary, paleozoic,* and doing it all so authoritatively. I was so deeply absorbed in this miracle that it was only as I was approaching the bottom of the first page that I became aware of what sounded like suppressed gasps and hisses somewhere around me. I half-turned my head to my right and saw a large freckled hand frantically signaling me to slow down.

I looked up at an immense, pink, jovial face, the eyes huge and blue and unmistakably bloodshot behind abnormally thick glasses and the mouth distended in a broad, fraternal smile. In a split second the thing, the ultimate in improbability, was clear. There *was* somebody who knew even less geology than I did! My paper was being copied by the teakhead.

Somehow I managed to suppress my laughter at the expense of a violent coughing fit. The proctor in charge of the proceedings rose and poured a glass of water from a carafe and walked rapidly in my direction. I was thinking of poor Roger and his endearing finickiness about odds. And how I might now be dead or sold into slavery if anyone had taken my bet—to say nothing of the loss of my dime. I sputtered a little as I drank the water. "You have a bad cough," murmured the proctor. "You should see a doctor as soon as you can."

If I needed a doctor, the proctor needed the services of a first-class otologist. To the accompaniment of a full orchestra of dim, whistling sounds, irritable raccoonlike squeaks, and rumbling exhalations, like the somber bleats of a muted double bass, my Waterman raced on, relentlessly dogged by my newfound buddy. The thought suddenly occurred to me that I might well be accused of copying from this blob of ochre on my right. Like a careful lawyer I first prepared my opponent's case. In my mind's eye I could see the court stenographer's record of my cross-examination in the trial:

Q.—Did you ever attend classes in geology?
A.—No.
Q.—Do you know where these classes are held?
A.—No.
Q.—Did you ever buy a geology textbook?
A.—No.
Q.—Do you deny that you were under suspension?
A.—No.
Q.—And that your paper is therefore without existence under the law?
A.—No.
Q.—Would you say that it is possible to copy a paper that does not exist?
A.—No.

Q.—One more question. Do you deny that you are a Jew?

A.—No.

Q.—No further questions.

To add to the overwhelming weight of legal evidence, the teak-head was rich, handsome, athletic, and a goy among goyim—one might even say a super-goy. (His luck never faltered. He married a very rich woman and, like the hero in a fairy tale, became a pillar of the John Birch Society.)

In the middle of a paragraph I was seized by what the old Germans called a *Raptus* and wrote *"satis, superque, O fartiter in re,"** and trusted I had resolved my difficulties. A heartfelt groan and the sound of frantic pen scratching on my right came like music to my ears. My own Latin of course I left unscratched.

Despite these untidy delays and hindrances, I was the first to finish the examination. As I handed it to the proctor, he whispered, "Be sure and take care of yourself." The eyes of my doppelgänger, like a pair of inflamed, swiveling robin's eggs, followed me out of the room.

Long after I had received notice of my expulsion, I was summoned to the dean's office. The dean was a frosty-eyed old fellow named Frederick Sheetz Jones.

"What are you doing here?" he said. "You've been expelled."

"Really? This is the first I've heard of it," I said coolly.

"You mean you didn't get your notice of expulsion? It was sent to your post-office box."

"Do you suppose I'd be hanging around here if I knew I had been expelled?" I had raised my voice. This was not only impudent, it was imprudent—the dean's temper was legendary. He glared at me speechless with outrage, his pink complexion began to darken into a more sinister shade. And then, like a shadow, a look of bewilderment passed over his features. I had delivered the *passado* and the *punto reverso*—now the moment had come for the *hai*.

---

* The first two words mean "Enough, more than enough." The remaining words are from a famous line in Horace's *Odes*, in somewhat altered form.

I walked to the door with the studied casualness of an old-school actor preparing the ground for his exit line. "If I am to be expelled," I said, placing one hand on the doorknob, "I believe I am entitled to a written notice. Good morning, sir." I deliberately opened the door and walked out. If the large inkwell on the dean's desk had struck me in the back of the head, I might have been injured but not surprised.

Absolutely nothing happened, either then or afterward. I never heard any more of my expulsion. Perhaps this proves the wisdom of a successful and now handsomely retired old tart. "Youth goes, beauty goes, but tricks," she said, "last forever."

But like the little man in Aesop's fable, I had buttoned my coat firmly against the wind only to shed it under the sun. A paper I had written on the subject of Christianity came back marked "A++. For maturity of thought and terseness of style, the best paper I have ever had from an undergraduate. C.A.B."

I was electrified.* The initials were those of Professor Charles Allen Bennett, the head of the Department of Philosophy and one of the very few members of the faculty I admired. He was of course anything but a Yale man. He was Anglo-Irish and had been educated in Trinity College, Dublin. His course of lectures was frequently disrupted by severe attacks of asthma, and what with my own chronic delinquency, I heard him speak on comparatively few occasions. As I had never met him personally, I had to introduce myself when I came to his office to thank him for his kind words.

"They weren't written as a favor," he said drily.

---

* Only this first paragraph of the paper I wrote for Professor Bennett was still, and only barely, legible when it was found among my effects after my family home was broken up, following the death of my father; the rest had faded utterly:

> It is astonishing how many millions of people in the Western world profess the Christian religion. What is scarcely less astonishing is how few practice it. There is nothing ironic about this state of affairs. If the protracted slaughter, recently concluded in Europe, proves anything at all, it is that this religion, the ultimate flower of an austere, desert-bred civilization, is completely unsuited to the still savage tribes that occupy that continent.

"Well, I can't begin to tell you how much they mean to me. I would like to ask your advice, sir."

"No advice is worth the breath it takes to give it," he said. "Hadn't you better sit down?"

I was breathing hard as I sank into a chair. Having come rushing into his office in a state of near dementia, I found his cool, aseptic responses thoroughly deflating. With his opaque dark-brown eyes and his almost deadly pallor, he seemed at close range altogether more forbidding than I had expected. I felt suddenly frustrated and sad when, to my astonishment, he smiled and said, "What have you been reading?"

"Oh, just about everything but the Bible and the Constitution of the United States of America," I said. "All the dramatists, classical and modern. All the novelists—all the philosophers from Plato, through the French *philosophes* and the German bores, right down to Croce, Bergson, Russell, and even Harold Laski's *Problem of Sovereignty*. With the result that I feel more ignorant than ever. I'm neither rich enough nor dull-witted enough to endure this awful place, and I feel that I ought to get the hell out of here."

The smile on his face had grown broader as I spoke. "Why not go?" he said.

For a moment I sat there, almost stunned by the simplicity of his remark. I rose from my chair. "Thank you, sir," I said. "You must surely know how grateful I am." I gave him my hand. "Thank you and good-bye, sir."

"If I were the sort to offer advice," he added, "I would say—never have a master."

Barely two weeks later, I found myself in Paris, precariously perched in a cozy little apartment with a glorious view of the Madeleine, dead flat broke and happy as a lark.

It is quite true that within days after I left Yale I found myself dead flat broke in Paris. But it is also less than true. Actually, I had ten dollars. And in the same sense, I suppose, it is true that, like George Orwell, I was "down and out in Paris and London." But here too there is more poetry than truth. I was not down at all and certainly never out. The qualifying phrase is that I was "happy as a lark." That was the salient difference between Orwell and myself. He was grum, I was buoyant. Indeed, within a week after I found myself "on the ragged edge," I had what was for me a fabulous income, a delightful *maîtresse*, and seemingly, Paris at my feet. If I had only taken the trouble to acquire a *femme* in one of the fashionable *arrondissements* and a *midinette* or two in the more modest quarters of that town, I might have been able to pass for a French senator. This exquisitely preposterous state of affairs came about, not with the mathematical logic of a first-rate stage farce but with the chancy, subtler logic of temperament and circumstance.

My arrival in the capital of France was anything but orthodox. While I was still at Yale, I had read an account in the *New York Times* of the difficulties Americans were encountering in trying to send money to their relatives in the then "new" countries of Poland, Czechoslovakia, Lithuania, and Latvia. The postal conditions in those newly formed states were lamentably raw. Money orders simply disappeared, and cash disappeared even faster. When I discussed the matter with Karl Blaustein, a friend at Harvard who like myself found college life tedious, we almost spontaneously decided to risk a few dollars on an advertisement in the *Times*, offering to deliver money by hand to residents of those countries with a flat 50 percent fee for delivery. The response was immediate and almost overwhelming. If we had been patient and businesslike, we might have been able to secure enough commissions to enable us to travel like gentlemen. But then, on a hasty miscalculation, we decided we had enough money to get to Europe and back. So we booked passage and took off.

I saw Paris for the first time one beautiful spring morning under a luminous, heart-melting, pale-blue sky which promptly fell in on us. An hour spent with a bright young Czech consul revealed that travel conditions in eastern Europe were still chaotic, and even worse in the rural areas where so much of the money was to be delivered. It was clear that our fees were insufficient to carry both of us through such a difficult, time-consuming journey. And like greenhorns, we had succeeded in whipsawing ourselves. Having planned to spend a few days sight-seeing in Paris, we were improvident enough to pay a week's rent in advance for a little apartment on the Boulevard des Capucines. Now it was painfully clear that every day, almost every hour we spent in Paris would further deplete our capital and, at worst, jeopardize our mission. In this atmosphere of crisis, we resorted to pencils and scratch pads; out of a litter of paper covered with columns of figures came the decision for one of us to take off that very night while the other was to be left in Paris with a stake of ten dollars. We tossed a coin, and I lost. I think I produced a decent show of gloom as I saw my friend off.

After all, who would choose to go to Kapuczuiska or Psczek or even Upper Bratislava, when he could stay in Paris? Since my capital was so small and my French vocabulary even smaller, the prospect seemed all the more irresistible. In a daze of happiness, I walked all over the city. For me Paris was art and literature and history sprung into life. After four days of this blissful pilgrimage, my money had just about run out. With a five-franc note in my pocket I decided to spend the morning viewing some of the masterpieces Napoleon had stolen from the Italians.

In the Louvre I had my first personal encounter. A young woman said something to me, and I replied that I did not speak French. This seemed to please her, and in deliciously accented English she asked me if I had ever been in Tennessee. This question, asked by a creature with a complexion out of a portrait by Renoir, took me utterly by surprise.

"No," I said. "I wonder why you are interested in Tennessee."

"Ah," she said vaguely, "I have to go there. You are *Américain*. Surely you can tell me something about this place."

"All I know about Tennessee comes from popular songs."

"Ah, there are songs about Tennessee?"

"Oh, yes. But most of them are produced by writers of Russian-Jewish extraction, so I don't think they make reliable guides."

"But why do Russian Jews write songs about Tennessee?"

"I must tell you that is the first intelligent question I have heard since I came to France." At this point we both burst out laughing.

"I don't know a single soul here," I said. "I have a million questions to ask and nobody to ask them of. Are you free to go walking with me one day?"

"Perhaps. I am staying here with my aunt. Where do you live?"

"Across the street from the Café de la Paix." I took out my little scratch pad and wrote down my name, address, and telephone number, and then we said good-bye.

"My name is Françoise," she said.

From the Louvre I made my way to the Guaranty Trust Company, then on the Rue des Italiens, and asked to see Mr. Rousseau, the managing director. He was very much amused by my account of my visit to Paris. But I thought he would jump out of his striped pants when I asked him for a job as a doorman.

"Good God," he said, "I couldn't possibly have a Yale man tending a door."

"No doubt a Harvard man would do a better job," I said. "My trouble is that I haven't enough French to qualify for anything more ambitious. By the way, do you need a dog?"

"A dog? Are you actually engaged in selling dogs?"

"Not exactly, but I think I can furnish one. You see, Mr. Rousseau, I am very good at chasing cats, and I think I could manage to learn to crouch at your feet and await your commands. Besides all that, I am extremely intelligent. . . ."

It was the only time I ever saw a banker convulsed with laughter. He drew a card from his desk drawer, and wrote something on it. "Now," he said, as he handed it to me, "this will get you a guest membership at the University Club here, and that will entitle you to drop in any afternoon for a nice cup of tea. And very likely you'll meet people and perhaps you'll get a few dinner invitations." I thanked him and found myself on the street again.

To pass the time, I wandered into an upstairs billiard parlor across the road from the bank and discovered that it was a gambling place. There were perhaps a dozen professional *billardistes* who were engaged in a program of matches on which a crowd of spectators made their bets. The heaviest bettor and by far the biggest loser was a Polish baron, an arrogant but impressive-looking blond fellow with a hand-

Jed Harris, 1979

Del-Hagen Studios

Jed Harris at age 6 (top left),
at age 9 (top right),
at age 28 (right)

Vandamm

Harris at a rehearsal of *The Lake*, Martin Beck Theatre, December 26, 1933

Theatre Collection, The New York Public Library at Lincoln Center,
Astor, Lenox and Tilden Foundations

TIME

The Weekly Newsmagazine

JED HARRIS
He knows it leads.
(See THE THEATRE.)

Volume XII

Number 10

Time magazine cover, September 3, 1928

Reprinted by permission from *Time*, The Weekly Newsmagazine;
copyright Time Inc. 1928

some, straw-colored mustache and elegant cloth-topped shoes. From time to time he imperiously ordered cognac from the attendant, an Arab youth, who served him with what seemed to me an outrageous show of mock courtesy. As I started to leave after watching the Pole drop twenty-five hundred francs within an hour, the Arab boy rolled his eyes in the direction of the baron, tapped his forehead, and whispered, *"Idiot."* He laughed heartily when I said, *"J' ne parle pas francais."* I had noticed that he had once gone to the window and collected a bet, and it occurred to me that the games might be framed. When on an impulse I said *"Ivri?"* he nodded joyously, and we shook hands. (Ivri is the old Biblical word from which *Hebrew* is derived.)

I had learned Hebrew as a child, and I was now, for the first time in my life, able to put it to some practical use. Between fragmented French and pitiful forays into the Holy Language, I was able to verify my guess that at least some of the games might be framed. The only problem was to get some money to bet.

The solution turned out to be simple. At the cost of a bad half hour with the baron the following day, I was able to persuade him (in German) to let me direct his betting. As the compass needle seeks the magnetic North, I searched the eyes of Yakoob, my Algerian friend. He never failed me. By five o'clock in the afternoon, the baron had won forty-five hundred francs, and he gave me a thousand. I now offered to split my winnings with my benefactor, but he refused to take any of the money. "You are my brother," he said. (In time I discovered that Yakoob was putting one of his brothers through medical school in Vienna, that he had financed a chain of garages in Algiers for other members of his family, and that two of the competing billiard players were in his employ. His weekly income averaged well over ten thousand francs and at twenty-three, he was, at least by French standards, a millionaire.) What was far more relevant was that I now possessed almost ten times as much money as I had started with. And even if I was not a millionaire, I did manage to feel like a new widower, grave but satisfied.

And I felt more than satisfied when I returned to my hotel

and found a message that Françoise would be waiting for me at six o'clock at the Café de la Paix. After a cold shower I changed into my "good" suit on which I still owed a New Haven haberdasher twenty-five dollars, and topped it off with a light, English-made tweed coat on which I owed only fifteen dollars. The card Mr. Rousseau had given me, I threw away. I had had my fill of universities. Catching my reflection in the old-fashioned pier glass which stood by the door, I decided I looked rather sporting.

Over dinner at the *Restaurant Perigourdine* that night, I learned that Françoise was engaged to marry an American army major in Memphis, Tennessee, and that she had come to Paris to do some shopping for the event. I gathered that she was finding it difficult to face the awful prospect of leaving France. What she had been able to find out about Tennessee was evidently not alluring.

Having been slightly anesthesized by the unaccustomed pleasure of a bottle of Clos de Veugeot, I found all these disclosures rather cloudy and remote. Waiting for a taxicab, I was therefore only mildly shocked to hear Françoise say she thought she would like to stay with me. In my benumbed state, her remark seemed directed at somebody else, not at me. There had not been a single word and certainly not a gesture of affection between us. While just barely not a virgin, I had had virtually no experience of Women. I wondered vaguely if I would be providing the major with a license to shoot me. But at age nineteen the pale cast of thought is very pale indeed. One does what comes naturally.

So began my ascent to the good life. Providentially, Françoise's aunt had gone to Le Havre to stay with her sister, who was seriously ill. Between my commissions and my own winnings my income was soon far more than that of a mere French senator. We dined, night after night, in the best restaurants, saw all the best shows and operas. I tipped like a spendthrift and became a favorite of headwaiters, somme-liers, and doormen. I engaged chauffeured cars to take us everywhere. Sundays we drove out into the country and visited delightful inns for lunch. I encountered well-to-do people only too ready to invite me to join cozy little combines on the Bourse. The baron expressed a willingness to back any venture I might propose. I heard nothing, day and night, but talk of money. Even Françoise implored me to save my money and start a good business. On the whole I was finding life a little tame and monotonous. As the days and weeks went by, the great state of Tennessee seemed to grow smaller and more shadowy. I thought the time had come to go.

One morning I rose early and spent the better part of my money on presents for Françoise, Yakoob, and the baron. The only thing I bought for myself was a first-class ticket to London—my last taste of luxury for years to come.

In London I ultimately sank far lower than I had in Paris. But the dividends were higher. If Paris stirred my sense of beauty, London won my heart. After a week spent savoring the delights of that city of cities, I found myself, on what the British call a damp night, on the Thames embankment with a threepenny bit in my pocket. The night was not as hard on me as it was on my tweed topcoat, which gained in weight what it lost in chic.

My genius for miscalculation had not deserted me. When I set out for London, I did not have the slightest doubt that I would be able to get a job there. Now I found myself in a city where there were a million men out of work. The great majority of them were ex-soldiers. It had been their fate to be thrown into the bloodiest kind of battles under the leadership of the most fantastically stupid generals in the history of warfare, and then to be left by even more stupid politicians to make the best of their shattered lives in the streets of London.

(Exactly twenty-five years later, I was invited by Lord Rank to watch the great Victory Parade from the Promenade of the Marble Arch Theatre. The other guests, a stuffy, dessicated lot, wallowing in titles, looked like refugees from one of the more scathing drawings of Georg Grosz. And I had no reason to alter this impression as the great fabricators of the victory—Churchill, Montgomery, Mountbatten, and the air marshals—rolled into view. The applause from the Promenade was almost sickeningly languid and perfunctory. Then, following the palatial cars of the great, came a vast throng in shabby, threadbare clothes, many of them hobbling on crutches. And, suddenly, my fellow guests were on their feet, cheering and sobbing for Britain's fire fighters. "You saved England!" they shouted. "You saved England!" This completely unexpected show of feeling left me a little shaken, but not too shaken to forget to bet all the English money I had on the Labour Party in the election which lay a few days ahead; an election that made sure that Britain's soldiers would get decent, humane treatment when they got back home. The world, as Bruno defiantly proclaimed, does move. But how slowly and at what cost.)

By the time I had walked up Villiers Street to the Strand, then past Trafalgar Square to Leicester Square, my coat, miraculously dried out, had resumed its natty aspect. I was on my way to a YMCA hut across the road from the Empire Theatre, where ex-servicemen could drop in for a cup of tea for tuppence. This treat, enjoyable as it was, reduced my capital by two thirds. Later a sturdy little Yorkshireman stood me to another cup. (Americans at that time were rather exotic types to the British.) We got into a friendly conversation, in the course of which he asked me if I was any good at crooking. He took it amiably enough when I said, "No experience and probably no talent." When he asked if I was "on the scrounge" and got a most emphatic affirmative, he said, "If you haven't got a bed for the night, meet me at the Y opposite Victoria Station." Then he went off with a pal called Blackie, who had distinguished himself with the Black Watch, an elite Scottish regiment.

Having spent the night on a cot in a huge shed that provided lodging for two hundred men at a shilling apiece, I discovered that my benefactor, Jimmy Hamilton, had adopted me. After paying for my breakfast in the canteen, he left with a promise to look me up later in the day at the Leicester Square hut. By the time he got there, I was face to face with a social problem. Some of the guests had staked me to a few pennies so I could play poker with them. They lost almost seventeen shillings, which left them penniless. Nevertheless, they were very much offended when I refused to take the money. Things were getting tense when Jimmy arrived.

"Jimmy," I said, "do you know any more blokes who might need a bed tonight?"

"Christ, yes. Dozens of them."

"Then take this," I said, pushing the money over to him. "There's enough to accommodate at least a baker's dozen."

"Right-ho, Yank," said Jimmy. "And bloody welcome."

He not only distributed the money but told everybody where it came from. The incident caused something of a sensation. And for the rest of the time I spent in London, I had what amounted to a couple of squads of security troops who considered themselves duty bound to look after me.

For the sheer sake of existence, most of the fellows I counted as friends had been drawn into petty crime: shoplifting, pickpocketing, and the occasional rolling of a drunk. I was especially taken with a pair of angelic-looking identical twins who stole pet dogs from old ladies and collected the reward after the victim advertised in the lost-and-found column. But if she was careless enough to betray strong emotion at the recovery of her pet, her address was carefully noted, and not long afterward she would find herself compelled to advertise again. They operated in the highest tradition of modern business, with a sporting indifference to anything but the bottom line.

(None of my friends ever committed a crime of violence. Not one of them ever carried a gun. My closest buddies, Jimmy and Blackie, were burglars. They spent days and sometimes long nights staking out their objective and moved only when certain of the results. But apparently not absolutely certain. Thus, a few days before I returned to America, they were caught breaking into a house in Golders Green, and were lodged in Brixton Prison, where I went to bid them good-bye and, incidentally, to pick up my tweed coat which Jimmy had borrowed on the night the police nabbed him.)

Our social center was the Swiss Café, a restaurant with a perfect view of the filthiest-looking object in London—the back of the Charing Cross railway station on Villiers Street. This was the Savoy Grill of the underworld, a place in which I felt very much at home. Considering that it was full of whores, ponces, thieves, and assorted knockabouts, the tone of the establishment may be described as sedate. The patrons really behaved like ladies and gentlemen. Although they lived precariously, these people seldom talked about money except as a wry joke. If you had a bit of money, you spent it on booze or friends or women, and when it was gone, you simply looked around for more. It was a Hogarthian world as it might have been filtered through the imagination of W. S. Gilbert or John Gay.

It now came to me like a marvelous discovery that I had lived for months without money, without women, without privacy, without even a decent bed. And yet I had thoroughly enjoyed my life in the company of these tough, kind, good-humored, and utterly abandoned people, as I could not enjoy the good people I had known in Paris. Was it merely a taste for low life? Or was it perhaps an early childhood influence? Two little friends of mine, the sons of a militant socialist on our block, used to parade around the playground, singing, "The middle class is a pain in the ass."

It would remain an essential element in my life: a feeling of ease with the best and rarest spirits in the world, or among the lowest of the low. It was only the middle range of society that often left me baffled, impatient, and hostile. That this polarity in my nature was the common property of adventurers and artists was something I would learn later on.

Discussing the matter one day at lunch with John Barrymore, he laughed and said, "I can't tell you how much this reminds me of my old man."

There was a feeling of kinship between Barrymore and myself. Born with a natural talent for the theatre, we had both tried to avoid it. And then, having succumbed to it, we had both achieved a high degree of success, without ever learning to come to terms with it. At the age of nineteen Jack was working for the New York *Evening Journal* as an apprentice cartoonist. (Lionel at the same time was studying painting in Paris. Neither of them had much interest in the theatre.) Jack was earning fifteen dollars a week and was perfectly happy in his work. But Ethel, who was herself a full-fledged star at the age of twenty-one, was pressing him hard to go on the stage. So he finally decided to consult his father, the elegant and hopelessly diseased actor Maurice Barrymore, who was living in the Lambs Club.

"My old man was still in bed when I got there," said Jack. "When I put the question to him, he got out of bed, lit a cigarette, and paced the floor. All he had on was a short pajama coat. He just puffed on his cigarette and kept scratching, rather fondly, I thought, on the biggest pair of balls I have ever seen. 'I'm sorry, my boy, I can't be of much help,' he said. 'You'll just have to make up your own mind. Either be a painter and putter or an actor and fornicate. In between the two, there seems to be nothing worth thinking about.'"

Unfortunately, I did not have the time to explore these guidelines of Maurice Barrymore's. But I was not too busy to become aware that success had somehow improved my looks. As a child I felt a secret kinship with the Ugly Duckling. Now suddenly, I heard myself described as "interesting looking." And as I produced more successes and acquired more money, I saw myself referred to as "striking" and, ultimately, even "fascinating." Whatever reservations I had about this extraordinary metamorphosis, a friend, a hard-headed* businessman, assured me that the change was real. "It is a cold fact," he said, "that the rich are better-looking than the poor." I wondered if that might be true.

Then I recalled the first time I ever saw Lynn Fontanne on the stage, in a charming comedy called *In Love with Love*, by Vincent Lawrence. Besides her gifts, she had what some people considered a big nose, and she walked badly. A woman sitting next to me dismissed her as an English clodhopper. But then Alfred Lunt fell in love with her and assured her that she was a beauty. Soon she began behaving like a beauty, and in a few years she was universally regarded as a beauty. The catch is that by that time she had far more money than she had the first time I saw her.

---

* Later, an ex-wife of his, a notoriously short-tempered lady, showed me a broken croquet mallet to prove it.

❧ THE WORM IN THE APPLE ❦

IF THE PATH TO FASCINATION NOW GAVE AN EDENLIKE quality to my existence, it was essential that a serpent should appear. And sure enough a tender little snake did turn up one day in the form of a suit for 50 percent of the profits of *Broadway*. The plaintiff, Leonard Blumberg of Philadelphia, claimed that he had met me during the tryout of the play in Atlantic City, and I had accepted his offer to finance the production with the understanding that I would call on him to provide the capital. Although he had the money, ready and waiting, I failed to get in touch with him. Since his backing would entitle him to half the profits from the production, he brought an action based on our "understanding."

I responded to this exactly the way I did when I had my pocket picked. I knew perfectly well that there were pickpockets, but it never occurred to me that they might operate on me. In the same way I was aware that nuisance suits often follow in the wake of big commercial successes in the theatre, yet I was naive enough to be astounded by the action. I shall confront death, I suppose, in very much the same manner.*

All I knew about the law I had learned from an old Senator from Missouri: "The law, the law!" he said. "How sinuous in its absurdity, how absurd in its sinuousity." But, as to be expected, Shakespeare said it best of all: "First ... let's kill all the lawyers."

If I was astounded, I was also amused. But Crosby Gaige, my financial partner, was utterly frightened.

---

* The last words of a friend of mine, a film producer, were: "Can this be happening to Pascal?"

"What did you say to Blumberg in Atlantic City?" he asked. He looked so scared that I could not help laughing.

"I will give it to you word for word. I said, 'Hello, Leonard, how are you?' He said, 'Fine. And you?' 'Just fine, thank you.' 'Have you all the money you need for this show?' he said. 'Yes,' I said. 'Well, if you find yourself short, I will be glad to help,' said Blumberg. I said, 'Thank you, Leonard, that's very nice of you.' That is a verbatim account of our conversation."

To my astonishment, Gaige said, "This is a very serious matter, Jed."

"This dialogue of ours is beginning to sound like Moran and Mack," I said. "The whole thing is so silly that I would be perfectly willing to go into court without a lawyer and offer Blumberg every chance in the world to prove his case."

"That is sheer madness," cried Gaige. "You must get a lawyer and a damned good one."

As I was now heavily involved in preparations for the rehearsals of *Spread Eagle*, I left it to Gaige to select the damned good lawyer of his choice. And I was shocked when it turned out to be Nathan Burkan, a renowned criminal lawyer whom I would have picked to get me off if I had committed a murder. (I did not know that he had a very considerable clientele in show business. One of his clients was his friend Victor Herbert, with whom he created ASCAP.) I argued that Burkan would assume that I had come to him because it was a difficult case, whereas it was in fact a very simple one. But "wiser" heads prevailed. Burkan agreed to take the case, and I had the novel experience of writing a check for $5,000, which was his fee. He asked for all the correspondence I had ever had with Blumberg, and the folder was delivered to his office within the hour.

A rather chilling, slab-faced bachelor in his fifties, Blumberg was the Shuberts' general manager in Philadelphia and the backer of my first two stage productions. His total investment in the two ventures came to $9,000, and he had reaped a profit of some $22,000. But he had driven hard bargains with me, so I had decided to seek backing elsewhere for *Broadway*. Since I felt that he could not hope to win this feeble, obviously trumped-up suit, I was mystified by his motive for bringing it. But I was much too busy to speculate on the matter. Having given Burkan an exhaustive account of our business relations and turned over all my records and correspondence, I expected to hear no more about it until we went to court.

The next day Burkan dropped into my office and said, "Are you sure that this folder you sent me contains everything that ever passed between you and Blumberg?"

"Of course."

"Frankly," he said in what I took to be an aggrieved tone, "I can't find anything in this correspondence that would be in the least helpful to Blumberg."

"Well, am I supposed to break down and cry?"

"I can't help wondering if there isn't something somewhere in your personal correspondence that might have gone astray or possibly been misfiled. There is nothing in the folder but business letters."

"I have never had any personal relations of any kind with Blumberg. We have never had dinner or lunch or even so much as a cup of coffee together. I have never discussed books with him, or music or women or even baseball. From what little I've seen of him I would say he's cold, ignorant, and without any interests whatever apart from money."

"Well, he's got William Klein, a very shrewd lawyer. I can't believe that Klein would go into court with a case that looks so weak. They must have something they're counting on. That's why I thought I'd come over and see if there might not be something you may have neglected to include."

"Mr. Burkan, are you suggesting that there might be something I haven't disclosed? That there is a letter or a document of some kind that I have withheld?"

"I was not suggesting anything. I just can't remember when I have felt so completely in the dark about a case. I'm sure that Klein has something to bring out in court, and it galls me not to be able to figure out what it might be."

"Why don't you drop out of this case, Mr. Burkan?" I said. "Take as much as you think you are entitled to out of the fee I paid you, and I will be perfectly satisfied to engage a very ordinary lawyer who won't subject me to this tedious and pointless kind of cross-examination."

"My dear boy, I'm only trying to protect you. I would be remiss in my duty if I didn't make every effort to find out what their case is based on."

"The key figure here is not Leonard Blumberg," I said. "It is Lee Shubert. It is his lawyer, William Klein, who is representing Blumberg. He could not possibly act in that capacity without the consent of the Shuberts. I believe it goes further than consent. I think it's a direct instigation."

"But why in Heaven's name would Shubert want to do anything like that?"

"Do I have to tell you what a stranglehold the Shuberts have on this business? They've cowed just about everybody on Broadway except me. In a couple of transactions I've had with them, I not only stood up to them but beat their brains out into the bargain. That's something they can't forgive, and this suit is just their idea of getting back at me. In England they wouldn't dare bring an action like this because they would have to reimburse the defense for all the costs. Klein is a salaried employee of the Shuberts, so the suit costs them nothing. It's a free country, Mr. Burkan, and especially free for shysters."

Burkan nodded thoughtfully. "I think you may have something there." He reached over and shook my hand. "You're a bright young fellow," he added, "and I think we'll do all right."

I got to the courthouse at ten minutes before nine. Burkan crossed the hall and drew me aside.

"I can settle this case for $5,000," he said. "And I urge you to accept this offer so we won't have to walk into that courtroom."

"I wouldn't settle this case for a nickel."

"My dear boy, a courtroom is an arena. It's like a jungle. Once you go into it, you never know if you're going to come out alive."

"I paid your fee, Nathan. Now go in there and do your stuff."

Burkan threw up his hands. "All right, if you're sure it's what you want. Five thousand dollars is peanuts."

"I'm not giving away any more peanuts."

The doors of the courtroom were now opened, and we entered the "arena." In a few minutes the trial was under way, and Blumberg was on the stand. Burkan had furnished me with a legal pad and a pencil and asked me to make notes of any misstatements Blumberg might make. It is only fair to admit that Blumberg gave his name, address, and the nature of his employment quite accurately. Thereafter, he lapsed into a stream of errors and trivial lies. I was not accustomed to getting out of bed at seven thirty. I was drowsy and bored with the proceedings. I stopped making notes and was beginning to doze off when I heard something that startled me.

Blumberg had testified that he had never bothered to read the manuscripts of the plays he had financed for me; he professed absolute faith in my judgment. Then Burkan showed him a letter he had written to an out-of-town theatre manager recommending that he book my first play. "I have read the script," he wrote, "and think it is very good." Blumberg readily acknowledged he had written the letter and that he had indeed read the script. But, he added with a patronizing little smile, he had not read the *manuscript*.

There was a moment of silence in the courtroom. William Klein, who looked like a starved coyote, raised his hands and clasped his head like a man bereft. The knuckles of Burkan's hands, gripping the rail, turned dead white. I felt sick.

Burkan now asked him quite pleasantly to explain the difference between a script and a manuscript. "Well," said Blumberg after some reflection, "one has dialogue but no stage business, while the other has both." Which, asked Burkan, had which? By the time we recessed for lunch, Blumberg was floundering like a beached whale in a morass of definitions, distinctions, explanations, and contradictions. Burkan said, "I will have this louse in the hospital before the day is out."

After lunch, Burkan went right back to the difference between scripts and manuscripts. By four thirty, Blumberg had broken down and was taken to Polyclinic Hospital. The case was abandoned.

The next day I had a telephone call from Lee Shubert.

"I hope you don't think we had anything to do with that suit of Leonard's," he said.

"The thought never occurred to me," I said. "I took William Klein's appearance for Blumberg as a coincidence."

"Bill and Leonard are old friends. They thought they had a good case, and I didn't feel we had any right to interfere."

"It was kind of you to call me, Mr. Lee," I said. "By the way, how is Leonard?"

"I understand he's much better today. I'm going over to see him this afternoon."

"Please give him my regards."

I came out of this affair determined to steer clear of lawyers and courts. So I became a devout supporter of the American Arbitration Society. I would sign no contract or agreement with anyone for any purpose whatever without an arbitration clause. Except for Ducks Unlimited, a nonprofit organization devoted to the preservation of these beautiful creatures, I never joined any group but the Arbitration Society. But, in keeping with the pattern of my life, I had again miscalculated.

One day, several years later, I was asked to appear as an expert witness in an arbitration between the late John C. Wilson and Metro-Goldwyn-Mayer. It would mark my first direct experience with the society, and I welcomed the opportunity. But I was again obliged to turn up at nine in the morning. And once again I arrived in a drowsy state. And I was revolted to see two banks of lawyers arranged on opposite sides of a long table. The arbiter was the president of the Equitable Life Insurance Company. And the "arbitration," I was dismayed to learn, had already been in session for two days. And, as I might have expected, the air was soon foul with cries of "Objection!" "Irrelevant!" and "Immaterial!" If I had only carried a grenade in my pocket, I might have been tempted to pull the pin and lob it where it might have done the most good. However, I gritted my teeth and listened to this bizarre nonsense for almost fifteen minutes. Then I rose from my chair, got my hat, and started to leave the room.

"Where are you going, Mr. Harris?" asked the arbiter.

"Home."

"But we are expecting to call on you in a little while."

"I'm sorry," I said, "but I won't sit here and listen to this crap. I joined this society under the impression that we were going to rid ourselves of these tiresome courtroom gambits. I will stay only if you will call on me without further delay. I think I understand what this affair is about, and I am ready to say what I have to say and then get the devil out of here."

"Very well," said the arbiter. He turned to the lawyers. "If you gentlemen agree, we will now call on Mr. Harris."

"First," I said as I took my seat again, "I will take the liberty of stating this case as I see it. Wilson produced this play, *The Day Before Spring*, in partnership with MGM. The play was presented in New York with indifferent results. While it wasn't a flat failure, it wasn't doing profitable business. There were losses in which both partners shared. Mr. Wilson then moved the production to Chicago, where it was a disastrous failure. But while MGM shared the costs and losses in New York, it has refused to pay its share of the losses in Chicago. MGM takes the position that since the play was a failure in New York, it should not have been transferred to Chicago. And MGM further places the full responsibility for the losses incurred on Mr. Wilson.

"I will not bore you with accounts of plays that succeeded in New York and failed in Chicago, nor the far more numerous plays that were successful in Chicago with contrary results in New York. I will merely add an item from my own experience. I once press-agented a show that cleared about $150,000 during its Chicago engagement, only to die in a single week in New York.

"Perhaps MGM has a good argument that the show should not have been sent to Chicago after its failure in New York. But that is based entirely on hindsight. And it would seem to me that MGM ought to win this case hands down, providing it can offer some evidence that, if the play had been successful in Chicago, MGM would have refused to share in the very considerable profits that might have come from a successful engagement. Short of that, I think it is the plain duty of the arbiter to rule in favor of Mr. Wilson. That is all I have to say."

I then went back home to get more sleep. Within ten minutes after my departure, the arbiter had rendered his decision.

Just before I fell asleep, I had a call from a Mr. Margolies of the MGM legal staff. "You murdered us" he said, "but I would like to congratulate you on the way you did it."

"I suppose I ought to thank you. But I think I should tell you that Jack Wilson is no friend of mine. On the other hand, Nicholas Schenck and Bob Rubin of MGM are both my very good friends. So I wasn't out to murder anyone. You had a lousy case and deserved to lose."

And so I stopped paying dues to the Arbitration Society. But I still clung firmly to my ducks. After all, one must somehow believe in something.

The collapse of Blumberg gave me no satisfaction whatever. Indeed, I had once again lapsed into my old freshman state, brooding endlessly on the whole sordid encounter with Blumberg. It was of course the perfect symbol of everything I tried to run away from. Now the days I had spent on the road seemed, in retrospect, like the most beautiful and rewarding time of my life. During that happy period I had hardly ever thought of the theatre and certainly never of the show business. Why then had I given up a world without greed, without vanity, without conniving shysters and droning judges, and returned to Broadway like a dog returning to his vomit?

The answer lay inside a beige-colored, collapsible old plastic file, resting on the green baize cover of my writing table, almost obscenely bulging with manuscript copy and resembling nothing so much as the carcass of a fat old cow, mischievously dumped on somebody's front lawn. Much of what appears in these pages had been extracted from that unappetizing-looking file, and now I removed a memoir I had written a quarter of a century ago. Here it is under its original title:

"How I Might Now Be a Retired Tycoon in Nebraska, If I Had Only Taken Advantage of the Breaks."

While traveling west late one night on a crack Chicago–Denver express, my teeth were clacking like typewriter keys and my body was shaking like a man in the last stage of palsy. Odd as this may seem, the explanation is simple. I was not inside the train but standing, exposed to the elements, directly behind the tender, my heels dug into the narrow threshold of the "blind"* front door of the baggage car, a perch made a trifle more secure by a vertical handhold around which my arm was curled.

It was an unseasonably cold spring night, and I was not properly attired for it. A thin, worn cardigan under my jacket was my only concession to the hazards of the weather. What worried me most was that I had lost all feeling in my legs, and I wondered if this might be the beginning of frostbite. Suddenly I could make out a vague blur of light far to the west. For a moment I felt a surge of relief—we were approaching McCook, Nebraska, a small town, probably stone dead at one o'clock in the morning. So it might be tough to find shelter for the night. But just to get off that train and out of the cold wind would be heaven.

The train had begun to slow up, and I was getting ready to jump off about two hundred yards from the station, a precaution necessary to avoid encounters with railway police who could be very rough with tramps. I was not sure my legs could stand the shock of the jump when I "hit the grit," but things turned out to be not as bad as I feared. Though I felt as if I had landed on a pair of stilts, I found I could walk. Then, from the darkness, I heard a voice.

"All right, young fella, keep moving. You're going out on that train tonight."

"The hell I am," I said. "I'm half-frozen now."

A burly man with a badge on his coat had materialized out of the shadows.

"I'm the sheriff here, and I say you're going out."

"Then you'll just have to arrest me," I said. "I don't mind spending the night in jail."

"Nothing doing. Jail's all full now."

He took a firm hold of my arm, and we continued to walk alongside the tracks. It was standard at the time for small-town police to keep vagrants moving on. As we approached the station, I could see smoke drifting up from the chimney and the windows of the little building shone with the rosy reflection from what I imagined to be a red-hot, potbellied

* "Blind" because it was not a door but a fraudulent architectural feature, a caprice of the designers of baggage cars.

44   A DANCE ON THE HIGH WIRE

stove. The rapidly diminishing prospect of warmth and shelter was almost too much to bear.

"Look," I said, "why not be a good fellow and let me spend the night in the station? And I'll be hitting the road first thing in the morning."

"You're wasting your breath. You're going out right now."

We were about a hundred yards beyond the station. And the train, behind its glaring headlight, was now moving again. Despite the blinding aftereffect of that monstrous light, I reached practiced fingers toward the handhold on the back end of the tender and drew myself up to the blind. Then, as the train picked up speed, I jumped off on the other side and hid between a couple of freight cars on the adjoining tracks. As the train slid past me, I could see the sheriff walking back toward the station. But instead of going in, he turned sharply left and disappeared from view. I now moved in the direction of the station myself, and soon I could make out the dwindling figure of the sheriff almost a long block away.

As I darted across the tracks toward the station, my heart was cold with the fear that it might be locked for the night. But the door yielded at a touch. The inside was dark except for the pink glow from the isinglass window of the stove. For a moment I stood there with my back to the wall in a state of perfect bliss. Then I sat down on a bench in the darkest corner of the place and was almost instantly asleep.

The station was still empty when I awoke a little after seven in the morning. As I opened the door to go out, I barely avoided bumping into a startled clerk on his way in.

"Good morning," I said. "Beautiful day."

"Morning," he muttered and disappeared.

It was indeed a beautiful day. As I walked across the street, a young boy was sweeping out a barbershop.

"May I use your soap and water?" I said. "I've got a safety razor, and I can shave in two minutes."

"Gee, I don't know," said the boy nervously. "The boss will be coming in any minute now."

Exactly three minutes later I was walking out of the shop and shaking hands with the arriving barber.

"Can I get a haircut around four o'clock?" I said.

"Sure thing. I'm open till six."

"Thank you, sir," I said. "I'll be there."

The morning sun shone out of a cloudless sky as I walked up the street. I smiled as I saw a big sign: "ATHENS WE NEVER CLOSE," and stepped into the restaurant.

"What can I get for a quarter?" I said to the sturdy Greek behind the counter.

"Ham and eggs, home fries, toast an' alla coffee you can drink. Okay?"

"Okay."

When I sat down to my breakfast, I had visions of being on the highway within half an hour, heading west. With luck I might get into Colorado that night. The Greek eyed me speculatively.

"Where you from?" he said.

"New York," I said.

"New York, heh? I never seen the place. I landed in New Orleans."

"That makes us even. I've never seen New Orleans."

"Where you bound for?"

"China."

"China! What's in China?"

"Lots of Chinamen, according to what I hear. By the way, who owns that empty lot next door?"

"Why you ask?"

"I've been knocking around for almost a year. And if I learned one thing, it's that the country is automobile crazy. And the roads are mostly lousy. So it stands to reason that they'll have to be modernized and that will increase the number of cars. And here you are about halfway between Omaha and Denver, smack in the middle of the U.S. And a natural spot for a layover. You could build a garage on that lot and service and wash the cars. That would make a profitable little business. A few billboards on the road are all you need to advertise the place. And with a restaurant on the premises, you'll be in clover. Of course if you can manage it, you ought to consider making the garage a two-story affair with maybe half a dozen rooms upstairs. That would be a great convenience for the travelers, getting their food, lodging, gas, and repairs all in the same spot."

The Greek was staring intently at me. I had finished my

breakfast and was draining my coffee cup. That back in 1921 I had casually invented the motel did not occur to me.

"Here," he said, "let me get you another cuppa coffee." He refilled the cup. "You know something? You make a helluva lot of sense," he said. "Why don't you stay here for a couple days?"

"I have to get out of here fast," I said. "Your goddam sheriff will be on my ass."

"Why? Whatsamatter?"

"I blew in on a blind last night, and he thought he'd got me out on the same train. So he'll be sore as a boil if he finds me here."

"Don't worry about him," said the Greek. "Sheriff's a good friend of mine. He owes me plenty favors."

"Anyway I just blew most of my capital on this very good breakfast. So I have to keep moving."

"You mean you're broke?"

I laughed. "If I had money yesterday and lost it, I'd be broke today. But I didn't have any money yesterday, nor the day before that, so I don't feel like a fellow who is broke. You wouldn't ask a man who has been coughing for a solid year if he'd caught a cold. Well, I must be pushing off."

As I rose from my seat, a snappy little man came in and said, "Give me a cuppa coffee, Alex. You don't know where I can get hold of a fella to dig some postholes out in the ball park?"

"Here's a smart fella," said Alex. "Maybe he'll do it for you."

"How much will you pay?" I was surprised to hear myself say.

"Fifty cents an hour. We want four holes, four feet deep. I furnish the tools. If you can start at eight this morning, I'll drive you out and then I'll pick you up at four o'clock. You'd better take along something to eat."

"I'll make up a couple sandwiches and give you a couple bottles of Coke," said the Greek. "You can pay me when you come back."

It was not until I was on my way to the ball park that I began to reflect on the sudden impulse that had propelled me into this battered old car with a paper bag in my hand and a pick and shovel at my feet. I had no desire to lay my hands on four dollars and certainly no taste for digging holes in the ground. I had little concern for the Protestant work ethic, a natural consequence, I suppose, of not being a Protestant. After all, I had quit a perfectly good job as a theatrical reporter. I couldn't help wondering if I was getting tired of my life as a tramp.

But now we were at the ball park. Near the center-field fence four little stakes had been driven into the ground at intervals of six feet. In a matter of seconds I was alone with my tools and my sandwiches.

I had never used a pick and shovel, and I was astonished to find the ground so hard. I had not been provided with heavy work gloves, so by the time I had dug the first hole my hands were quite sore. It was noon when I had finished the second hole, and my heart was full of pity for all the gravediggers in the world. It was a very warm day, and I was violently hungry. I wolfed the sandwiches and Cokes Alex had given me. Despite an aching back and blistered hands I somehow managed to finish the job as my boss came to fetch me. He took a quick look at the work, grabbed the pick and shovel, and said, "Fine. Jump in." He paid me the four dollars and drove me back to Alex's place.

Alex brought me a dish of roast beef and mashed potatoes. When he saw my hands, he took me back to the kitchen and applied a slightly astringent creamy-looking lotion that he kept in a milk bottle. And the condition of my hands was improved almost immediately.

"Tricks in every trade," said Alex with a smile.

When I had finished the meal, I tried to pay him what I owed, but he waved the money aside.

"I made an offer for that lot this afternoon," he said.

"That's marvelous, Alex," I said. "I'm sure it's something you'll never regret."

"I wanna talk to you tonight, after the rush is over. I went over to see Mrs. Hatch around the corner. She's got very nice furnished rooms. I told her to expect you. I paid her a week's rent in advance."

"You're a sweet son of a bitch, Alex. But I'm sure I won't be staying here a week."

"You never know," said Alex. "Wait till we talk tonight."

"Alex," I said, "I hope you won't mind if we put off talking till tomorrow. I'm just too damned tired."

"Fine," he said. "I'd rather see you have a good night's rest."

I looked at the clock and suddenly remembered the barbershop. So I went over and had my hair cut. The sheriff came in shortly afterward and sat in the next chair. We looked at each other in the mirror.

"Hello," I said.

"Oh, hello," he replied politely. He kept staring at me.

"Nice town you got here," I said.

"I guess it's all right. Where are you from?"

"San Francisco. I stopped over here to see Alex."

"Oh, you a friend of Alex?"

"They don't come any better."

The barber was removing the cloth from my neck. In the mirror I could see that I had picked up a coat of tan in the ball park, although there was a bit too much pink in it for my taste.

"You live in McCook?" I said affably to the sheriff as I paid for my haircut.

"He's the sheriff," said the barber with a laugh. Then, seeing that I had given him a tip, he said, "Thank you. Thank you, sir. Never ran into anyone from San Francisco who wasn't a sport."

I went over and shook hands with the sheriff. "Excuse my ignorance, sir," I said.

"Oh, sure," said the sheriff. "It's all right."

Predictably, the sheriff was still staring at me through the mirror as I walked out the door. What is more to the point is that I could not stop staring at myself. My haircut and my coat of tan seemed to have transformed me. As I looked into the shopwindows along the main drag, I was doing exactly what I had done as a child of eight when I was blacked up for a school minstrel show and found it impossible to stay away from the mirror in the dressing room.

And no wonder. Barely fifteen hours ago I had arrived in McCook, miserably cold and hungry with some fifty cents to my name. And now I was a sporting gentleman from San

THE WORM IN THE APPLE   49

Francisco with money in my pocket, tanned and freshly barbered, with a generous patron and a furnished room and with that once inhospitable sheriff suddenly metamorphosed into a mannerly and respectful friend. And, even more miraculously, the pains and aches I had acquired in the ball park had all but vanished.

It was in this somewhat epic mood that I strolled into a noisy pool parlor. It was like the trading floor of some proletarian stock exchange. Two pool sharks were engaged in a match, pausing briefly after each shot, while a baldish little man with an apron pouch full of money called the odds, which shifted according to the difficulty of the shots, the length of the runs, and other factors too subtle for me to understand. The air was foul with smoke and the stink of rotgut whiskey (it was of course in the era of Prohibition). I ordered a Coke. Standing beside me was a disheveled young man, unsteadily pouring liquor out of a pocket flask into his own soft drink on the counter. In his other hand he clutched a fistful of bills. A half-chewed cigar rested on a filthy ashtray beside his drink.

"How are you doing?" I said.

"Never seen the like of it," he said in a tone of wonder. "I haven't lost a single bet today."

I took a dollar bill out of my pocket and handed it to him.

"The next time you bet, throw this into the pot, and see if you can win for me."

"Gee, I don't know. I might lose it for you." He took a long pull on his drink.

"I have a feeling you'll go on winning. I can see you're a clean-living fella. You don't drink, you don't smoke—"

He was choking on his drink as he was caught in a paroxysm of laughter. He wiped the dribbled liquor off his chin with his shirt-sleeve.

"The minute I laid eyes on you, I thought here is a future deacon of the Methodist church," I continued. This set him off again.

"Jesus Christ," he said, "now I gotta win for you. You wait here and keep an eye on my drink."

He moved into the mob of punters and returned in a

couple of minutes. And for the second time that day I was handed four dollars.

"I won and doubled the bet on two shots," he said. "I did all right too." He laid all his cash on the counter and began to sort it out. "This is going into the bank," he said. "I've been saving up for an Apperson Jackrabbit. Gimme another phosphate," he said to the bartender.

"When you're a deacon, you'll be riding in a Buick," I said as we shook hands.

I went next door and bought a shirt and tie and a pair of socks. Then I took a long shower at the local Yemka, as we called the YMCA when I was in the army. All these furnishings and amenities cost me 95¢.

Back on the street I was walking on air. It suddenly occurred to me that pool parlors, shady places I had been taught to avoid, had exercised a most benign influence on my fortunes. I just did not feel like being locked away in some furnished room, so I drifted back to Alex's place. He was astonished to see me.

"Did you have a nap?" he said. "How did you like Mrs. Hatch? You know, I almost didn't recognize you. You look like a different man."

"It just goes to show what a shower and a clean shirt can do for you," I said. "I stopped off at the Y." And he laughed when I told him of my encounter in the pool parlor.

"Let me tell you something. You're gonna get to like this town. The sheriff dropped in and mentioned he met my friend from San Francisco. I knew who that was, and I had a helluva job keeping a straight face. So I was right. You got no problem with the sheriff." He motioned to a table in the corner of the restaurant, and we sat down. His young cousin Stefan had come on for the night shift. He brought a couple of glasses, and Alex poured us some very smooth Scotch whisky from a small medicine bottle.

"You know, Marcy Hatch is a very fine lady," he said. "But you'll see that for yourself. As a matter of fact she's my wife's best friend. She lost her husband only a year ago, and I invested some of her insurance money for her in the house.

She's only been open for a month or so, but I'm sure she'll do all right." I wondered why he was telling me all this.

"Especially if you make a habit of paying room rent for every vagrant that hits town."

"If they were all like you, I'd consider it a good investment," said Alex. "Look, I wanna talk a proposition with you."

At this moment a tall, somewhat actorish-looking man carrying a valise came in.

"Hello, Alex," he said, putting his bag down on an adjoining table. "I've got to wash my hands. Will you order me a roast beef sandwich and some French fries?" He disappeared into the washroom.

"Who is he?" I said. "He looks like a performer."

"He's a travelin' salesman. He sells books. He's been around here a couple weeks."

When the man came back, Alex introduced us and I discovered that he was selling sets of *The Book of Knowledge* to the schools in the countryside. He showed us charts covering an area of some fifty miles around McCook, and it seemed he systematically went from one school district to another offering his wares. Each set was sold for seventy dollars and his commission came to eighteen dollars. He claimed to average four sets a week. Then he suggested I try selling a couple of districts. He had a car and would drop me off in the area I was to cover.

"Do I get eighteen dollars if I make a sale?" I said.

"No, I get an override of two dollars. But if you're lucky enough to make a sale, I'll pay you sixteen dollars."

He opened his bag and took out some brochures and a collapsible, accordion-pleated set of book backs.

"Now you read that stuff tonight, and I'll make you a good bet you'll know enough to make a pretty good pitch. And here's a manila envelope made especially for the book backs. Take my word for it—it's very impressive when you open it up. And don't forget, you have to get three signatures from the school board to make a sale. The trick is to get the first guy to sign. The second one is always easier. By the time you show the third guy you've got two signatures, he usually signs without a murmur. I'll meet you here at seven thirty in the morning and give you a list of the school-board members you'll be calling on."

"When do I get paid?" I said. Alex was smiling broadly.

"Well, Jesus, you haven't sold anything yet, and here you are demanding your money."

"And he's damn right," said Alex. "You oughta pay on the spot, if he delivers the goods."

"Well, if he makes a sale, he'll get paid right then and there," said the salesman. His name was Appleby. "*If* he makes the sale," he added.

I looked at the pile of promotional material with some distaste. And I did not like Appleby. But I said nothing. I picked up the stuff and said good-night to Alex.

"You must be damn tired," he said. "Have a good rest."

Mrs. Hatch turned out to be something of a surprise. When I rang her doorbell, she appeared almost immediately. She was wearing a satiny robe of some kind, and she was an attractive auburn-haired woman of thirty with good clear features and merry eyes.

"Alex called me up and said you'd be here by five o'clock. He told me enough about you to make me think you'd run off. I must say you don't look a bit like a man who spent the day with a pick and shovel. Are you hungry?"

I laughed. "No, thank you. I did do a little digging but outside of that I've done nothing but eat all day." I had followed her into her parlor, and there was an open book on the table. "What are you reading?" I said.

"*The Man That Corrupted Hadleyburg.* Mark Twain was my husband's favorite writer, and we bought the whole set of his books. And I've been going through them for the second time. None of the girls I used to go around with ever gave a hoot about Twain. They said he wrote strictly for men. But my husband got me started on *Life on the Mississippi,* and I've been hooked ever since."

"*Life on the Mississippi* is a darling book," I said, "but your friends were probably right. Mark was really at ease only among men. In his old age, in a speech at a smoker, he said, 'I don't know about you gentlemen, but as for me, I'd rather be alone and naked with Lillian Russell than to be with General Grant in full uniform.' "

Mrs. Hatch looked shocked for a moment and then shrieked with laughter. "Oh, the things those writers think of! Now that's a story I could never tell my mother." She began to laugh again. "For that matter I couldn't tell it to my father either. Well, I guess I'd better show you your room."

We went upstairs past the hall bathroom, and she flipped a switch as we entered the room, and a little pink-shaded lamp on the bed table cast a discreet glow on a very neatly arranged bedroom. From the expression in her eyes I was sure that Alex had played Cyrano for me. And she seemed to have grown even more attractive.

"Well, it's very nice, Mrs. Hatch," I said, "but I wonder what it will be like when you go back downstairs."

"I don't have to go down yet," she said and walked into my outstretched arms.

After we had kissed, she whispered, "Alex says you're the smartest fellow he ever met." We were quite alone in the house. Her other tenant was away in Hastings. "Let me go downstairs for a couple of minutes. Then after your light is out, I'll come back."

We made love half the night, and she woke me at six in the morning. Needless to say I had read none of the promotional literature I had been given.

Over coffee she told me how kind Alex and his wife Ella had been to her. I also gathered that I was the only man who had ever "touched" her since her husband's death. It had been a long time since I had "touched" anybody either. But I saw no reason to say so.

Before I went out to meet Appleby, I spent about twenty minutes going over his brochures. I was astounded to find the pitch for the books really persuasive, and I wondered why he hadn't been able to sell more of them.

Appleby had drawn a map of the area I was to cover, and I was studying it in the car as we drove off some fifteen miles from town. He had also drawn dotted lines to indicate the path I was to follow from one farmer's house to another.

"If you follow the lines I've drawn, you'll be walking about nine miles before the day is over. I'll meet you around twelve o'clock at the Zemanski farm to see how you're doing."

I was only half-listening to him. I was absorbed for the moment entirely in myself. Why the hell had I stayed on in McCook and why was I out here in this very sparsely settled country, doing something in which I really had no interest?

Dropped at the Rodenbach farm, I found the proprietor, a big fellow born in Bohemia, messing about in his stable. I went into my spiel, and I thought I made a very decent case for *The Book of Knowledge* as I reeled off the great benefits the children of his district would derive from it. Like one of his farm animals he merely grunted several times.

"I'll tell you the truth," he said. "If I signed this paper, you could never get the signature of Sigmund Knabe, because he hates my guts. All he's got to know is that I'm in favor of something, and that's enough to put him against it."

"But this is something to help teach the children around here. Why should Knabe make a personal thing out of it?"

"I'll tell you why. Because he's a mean son of a bitch, that's why. Now personally, I like the idea of getting these books for the kids, but I know we'll never get them if he sees my signature on the order."

"Well, suppose I get Knabe's signature, will you sign?"

"Yes, sir." He held out his hand. "I give you my word."

I showed him my map and the route that Appleby had marked out. "Is this the best way to get to Knabe's place?"

"You'd do better to cut straight through from my north field. It's shorter. 'Course it's a little upsy-downsy, but you'll save some shoe leather."

The country was on the edge of the foothills of the Rockies, and what Rodenbach quaintly called upsy-downsy had me climbing little mountains and descending into steep gullies. The farms in the area ran anywhere from three hundred to six hundred acres, so I got quite a workout.

Knabe, a good-natured German immigrant, was coming into his house for his second *Frühstick* when I got there, and his wife was setting his enormous breakfast on the table.

I wasted no time. After showing him the flashy accordion-pleated set of book backs and assuring him that his children would learn for the first time how matches were made, I said bluntly, "Mr. Rodenbach said you hate his guts and that if he signed the order blank, you wouldn't go along."

"Oh," he said lightly, "I guess you never met Rodenbach before. But you can ask anyone around here. Rodenbach is the biggest liar in the county and for all I know in the whole state of Nebraska. You go back and tell him I have given my word that if he signs, I'll sign."

"I believe you, Mr. Knabe, but I feel it would be hopeless to go back and tell that to Mr. Rodenbach. Why don't you write a note: 'To whom it may concern: if Rodenbach signs the order for the books, I will sign.'"

He took some time to think this over while I sipped coffee.

"Well, I see nothing wrong with that. Helga," he said to his wife, "get me a pencil, will you?"

She was bringing me some coffee cake and immediately got a pencil and a lined sheet of paper. The farmer wrote the note, exactly as I dictated it and signed it "S. Knabe."

I thanked them for their hospitality and started back to Rodenbach's. I figured that Rodenbach would say that Knabe would renege: "If he wanted the books, he would have signed the blank." I found a nice flat rock in one of the fields, sat down and very carefully forged Knabe's signature on the form. Rodenbach was obviously startled but made no fuss whatever about signing. Then on the way back to Knabe's farm, on my lucky flat rock once more, I erased Knabe's signature and once I showed him the form with Rodenbach's signature, he signed immediately.

Mr. Varney, the third member of the district board, whose farm I reached in another half hour, seeing the two signatures on the form, did not have to be sold at all.

"If these two fellows who can't say a decent word to each other, can agree on it, I'm for it no matter what the hell it is."

It was not quite ten o'clock, and I had managed to finish half my job. As luck would have it, Varney was bound in the direction I was to take for the next district, and he was kind enough to drop me off at Adolf Kleinhof's place. Kleinhof and an elderly man, Mr. Zemanski, both board members in the adjoining district, were having a convivial morning with some very strong home-made whiskey. I could not refuse the glass

A DANCE ON THE HIGH WIRE

they offered me. I somehow managed to drain it without any sign of discomfort. But I sat down very suddenly.

There was no question about "selling" *The Book of Knowledge* to them. On seeing the order I had taken from District 17, they signed without any prompting from me. I told Zemanski I was to be picked up at his place at twelve o'clock. After another round of drinks, he stopped at the third board member's house, took the form with him, and left me, only too grateful not to have to get on my feet, in the truck. I was beginning to feel sick. Zemanski returned in a few moments with the last signature. When he brought me back to his house, I sat down in his kitchen and dozed off.

I was awakened by Appleby's arrival and got into his car after bidding the Zemanskis good-bye. My condition didn't escape Appleby's keen eye.

"Have you been drinking on the job?" he said severely.

"What job?" I said. "I didn't take a job. Anyway, I'm quitting right now. I feel lousy and I want to get back to town. Here," I said, handing him my two order forms. "I've sold two sets, and I want my money. Thirty-two bucks."

"You say you sold two sets?" His tone was a delicate mixture of disbelief and outrage.

"There are the signatures."

"I don't believe it," he said.

I snatched the forms out of his hand and said, "Drive me back to town so I can be rid of you."

"Aren't you going to give me a chance to check out the signatures? That's standard practice."

"You called me a liar, you son of a bitch," I said.

"I did nothing of the kind. I just said it was unbelievable. That doesn't mean I called you a liar."

"I'm going to ask my friend Alex to throw you out of his place for being a cheat."

He was now thoroughly frightened. And I finally agreed to go back over my route to check out the signatures. I never got out of the car as he called on the various signees. Indeed I slept like a dog for the next hour.

When I came to, he apologized profusely for having expressed any doubts about the orders, and he handed me thirty-two dollars. On the way back to McCook he begged me to go into partnership with him.

"In the entire history of the Grolier Society," he said, "nobody ever made such a selling record." He even offered me a half interest in his car. I only shook my head and said nothing. He wanted to stop at Alex's, but I insisted on being taken to Mrs. Hatch's place. Apart from that, I had not spoken a single word to Appleby since our blowup. His overtures to me were left hanging in the air, and I only added to his frustrations when I suddenly decided to be dropped in the center of town, where I left him, thoroughly baffled, with the briefest of farewells.

In a tiny shop I had passed the day before, I bought a pretty Victorian cameo pin set in gold and a tie clasp, beautifully devised underneath a bar of lapis lazuli, also set in gold, and arranged for their delivery to Marcy and Alex.

Marcy was out when I got to the house a few minutes later, so I went upstairs, undressed, and got into bed. But I could not sleep. I was cursing myself for taking those vile drinks, to pass for a "good fellow" and make a sale. I had always hated the petty deceits that are the basis of salesmanship. So I lay there, tossing about in acute discomfort, masochistically aware that I was being justly punished for violating my ideals.

I had always seen myself as a kind of Julien Sorel in Stendhal's *The Red and the Black*. Now I was beginning to detect my disconcerting resemblance to Hlestakov, the amiable young scoundrel in Gogol's *The Inspector General*. I had passed rapidly through a series of impersonations as a business genius, an honest day laborer, and a superior book salesman. They say that wit, more often than not, comes at the expense of others, but humor reflects on oneself and is therefore healing. Anyway, I fell asleep.

I was awakened by a shout of laughter. That the laughter was my own did not altogether surprise me. I had just sat through a dress rehearsal of my production of Wycherly's *The Country Wife*, and I had been laughing all through the performance. And especially at the funny business I had devised for the leading characters.

I had been so deeply immersed in the dream that for a

moment I could not identify my surroundings. Then Marcy appeared with a steaming hot cup of coffee.

"I came up here fifteen minutes ago because I heard you laugh," she said, "and you were fast asleep. But I was sure you must be up after that last laugh. It was loud enough to wake the dead."

Her eyes were shining. She had stopped off at Alex's and heard Appleby's account of my heroic sales exploits with *The Book of Knowledge*. And I was amused to learn that Appleby had mentioned my unfortunate "drinking problem." But for that, he had assured Alex, he might have offered me a full partnership in his business.

"It must have slipped his memory," I said, "but he *did* offer me the partnership. He even offered me a half interest in his car."

"Why, the man is nothing but a common liar," she said indignantly.

"No, he's just a salesman. And his feelings were hurt when I ignored the offer." I had been looking around the room. "Where are my clothes?"

"Oh, I've been doing a little cleaning and pressing. We're invited to Alex's house for supper. I'll bring them up in a few minutes." She smiled. "Before it slips *my* memory," she said as she kissed me, "here's a down payment on my pin."

As I lay soaking in a hot bath, I marveled that my passion for the theatre, like the long-suppressed memory of some shattered love affair, had again taken possession of me. After all, I had only run away from the trivialities of show business, not from the theatre. And suddenly I could see what it was that had kept me staying on in McCook and occupying myself with little jobs: my tramping days were coming to an end. Indeed, the vividness of that dream gave me something I had never experienced before—absolute confidence in my feeling for the theatre.

Alex came to the door to welcome us when we got to his house. He was wearing a dark suit over a pale blue shirt with a starched collar and cuffs and looked altogether formal, as though our visit was an occasion. By contrast I looked like the hero of an Alger book, shabby but neat, in my well-brushed rags. He pointed to his new tie clasp. "I had to dress up if I was going to wear that thing," he said as he embraced me.

Ella was a pretty blonde, just beginning to turn plump. She was wearing a rather absurdly frilled apron over her dress. Indeed almost everything in the house was frilled or ruffled or pleated, as if it had been decorated by a fanciful little girl. But her manner was unexpectedly earthy.

"Alex," she said as we shook hands, "how did you say that madam in Omaha greeted her guests?"

"'All hookers, hashers, and hackies are welcome here,'" said Alex. "But I don't think that's the right thing to say just now, Ella."

"No—it's really insulting," I said. "Why should she discriminate against hoboes?"

The party had gotten off to a pleasant start as the ladies made for the kitchen, and Alex and I sat down in the parlor.

"By the way, I got some news for you," he said. "I talked to Bill Dobish this afternoon—he's the best builder around here—and he believes your idea is a winner. He's gonna bring an architect over from Lincoln to work out a plan for the building. But he thinks the place ought to look like an inn, not like a garage. He's for putting the garage in the basement, out of sight of the customers. So the whole thing can be one story with maybe ten or twelve rooms."

"He's damned right. He sounds like a really smart guy."

"Y'know, he's so crazy about the idea that he'd like to go partners with us on the deal." I was more than a little startled to find myself included in the affair. "And I'll tell you something else. He knows a couple of lots in Hastings that he thinks we could pick up for a song. So he's all for taking up a cheap option on the property. So if we do good here, we can start expanding—you know, like a chain. How does that hit you?"

"Right between the eyes, Alex. Your friend Dobish is even smarter than I thought. Now that's the kind of partner you really need."

"We might wind up with lotsa partners," he said mysteriously. Then, after a pause he continued. "What I been thinking about can't be done by one or two partners. It's gonna take real money. You know that song 'How You Gonna Keep

'Em Down on the Farm After They've Seen Paree?' Sometimes one of those songs tells you something. Like for instance there's an old farmer name of Zemanski. He had two children. The boy was killed in the war, and his daughter married a doctor in Pittsburgh. So he's gonna have to sell out and retire. And he's not the only one. More and more of these farms are gonna come up for sale. Most of those fellas are immigrants like me. Their children get a better education than they had, and they'd rather get away from the loneliness and the hard work on those farms."

"I know Mr. Zemanski," I said. "I slept in his house."

For a moment Alex looked so stupefied that I laughed. "It was on one of his kitchen chairs that I slept off part of my drinking problem."

"My God," said Alex, shaking his head. "It's hard to believe how everything fits. What I'm gonna tell you now is something that's been on my mind for a long time. A few years ago I staked Stefan's younger brother to agricultural college in Iowa. But practically from the beginning he began picking up scholarships, so it didn't cost me much. Well, he's gonna graduate next year. Over there they all think he's a genius. What they don't know is that he happens to have a great head for business. He tells me that the people from International Harvester are gonna be coming out with big machines that will do practically all the work on the farms. So if you can afford to buy the land and the machines, you can plant and harvest thousands of acres at a time and bring down your costs. You have to meet this kid, and he'll convince you that the idea makes lotsa sense."

As Alex went into the details of financing an agricultural empire of maybe thirty thousand acres, I was absorbed in blocking out five minutes of hilarious pantomime for the opening scene of *The Country Wife*. My pleasure must have shown on my face because it seemed to inspire Alex to draw a glowing picture of a giant corporation, centered on agriculture, hotels, garages, and restaurants, in which we would be major stockholders.

How many thousands of shares I would have acquired in that glorious conglomerate is something I never thought of at all. At six o'clock the following morning I caught a thirty-mile hitch going west. My feet were pointed toward New York, so I felt like someone walking backward. It was the first day of May, and there would be no jobs in the theatre as the season was about to sink into the doldrums of summer.

After we left Alex's house, I explained to Marcy just how matters stood with me, and she agreed to break the news to Alex. "It's the sort of thing I haven't got the guts to do," I said. "Alex is just too innocent to understand anyone who isn't interested in business and making money. But you do, and I know you'll do a good job of it."

Within a week I was living in the Brown Palace Hotel in Denver, wearing clothes appropriate to my status as editor of a weekly magazine devoted to the arts. I was getting fifty dollars a week and a generous expense account. Since I had appointed myself dramatic critic of the paper, I covered the bill on the opening night of the summer season of the stock company at Elitch's Gardens. The play was an English courtroom drama called *Butterfly on the Wheel*, and I was much taken with the performance of a young actor playing a barrister. He seemed to be the only member of the company who spoke good stage English. I sent my card backstage with an invitation to have a cup of coffee with me. Offstage he spoke like a thorough New Yorker.

"Why not stay on here after the summer season is over?" I said. "I think you're a hell of an actor. We'll form a company and do some really good plays."

"I'd love to do it, believe me," he said, "but I have a contract to play for Arthur Hopkins in the fall, and I'll be getting sixty dollars a week. My father is old and sick, and my first obligation is to see that he gets everything he needs."

His name was Edward G. Robinson. But no matter. I would arrive in New York in August to find that my debut as a producer and director of plays would encounter some very tiresome delays.

❧ A LONG DAY'S MORNING ❧

I HAD SPENT A LONG MORNING RUMMAGING THROUGH THE contents of that unappetizing-looking file on my writing table, and I needed a little diversion. So I turned to a copy of the magazine *Commentary*, a much-admired publication, devoted to high thinking and modish plugs for Hanukkah cards. What I wanted, however, was a little light reading, and that is to be found only in the Letters section. I was not disappointed.

There in the very first letter I found Professor Arthur Schlesinger, Jr., calling Professor Noam Chomsky a liar and a phony. It was as if Willie Mays had called Babe Ruth a honky with a shaved bat. (Of course modern ballplayers, trained in the arts of public relations, are incapable of such unrestrained language. Nowadays it is the professors who are the swingers.)

Briefly, Professor Schlesinger accused Professor Chomsky of deliberately misquoting a speech of President Truman's and then, even more deliberately, misinterpreting the misquotation. For a moment I lapsed into a state of shock. Grasping at straws, I struggled to remember whether this came under the legal doctrine of double jeopardy or the rule of grammar that two negatives make a positive. But when my brain had cleared, I thought: Dear God in Heaven, if eminent fellows like Chomsky can be guilty of tricks of that sort and, what is really scandalous, be caught out into the bargain, who the hell is there left to believe?

But somehow the thought of the "prestigious" professors engaged in an untidy row of this sort rather exhilarated me. And so I was quite cheerful when my telephone rang, and I was glad to hear a voice I had not heard for a long time.

"How are you, Ferdie?" I said. "I mean I really want to know how you actually feel."

"I'll give it to you straight. First thing I do when I get up in the morning, I open *The New York Times* to the second page of the second section and check the obits. Once I make sure my name isn't on the list, it gives me a hell of an appetite. I guess you can say I am doing as well as the average eighty-four-year-old. Maybe I even have an edge on some of them."

"It's just great to find you so chipper, Ferdie. How are the files?"

"Still blooming, believe it or not. For anyone who walked out of the theatre so long ago, your name keeps popping up all the time. By the way, do you know there was a magazine article that mentioned you had once taken an option to produce *The Fifth Column*?"

"Not really? Do you know who wrote it?"

"No, I didn't see the thing. I'm trying to track it down. A friend of mine said he'd heard of it. I told him I remember asking you to go to the opening, and you begged off because you'd read the play and thought it was a piece of junk. Which it certainly was."

The brisk tone of this conversation was altogether characteristic of other exchanges we had enjoyed over the years. A middle-rank functionary in the New York office of the Paramount Pictures Corporation, Ferdie Weill had, entirely without my knowledge, appointed himself my recording angel. He is probably the only person in the world who knows more about my theatrical career than I do. He has preserved masses of programs, photographs, reviews, and literally thousands of clippings. When I gave him my scrapbooks before taking off to California in 1940, he received them as if they were a princely gift. I once asked him why he bothered to keep all this rubbish. He shook his head sadly. "You're like Stokowski," he said. "He considers these things rubbish too. Let's just say I'm an old bachelor, and this just happens to be my hobby."

But of course I knew nothing of this hobby when I first met him over drinks in 1931 in the apartment of Joseph Schenck. And he did not ingratiate himself with me when he launched into an account of the opening night of *Broadway*. He passed lightly, I thought, over the merits of that superior melodrama. Indeed, for him the high point of the evening was not the play but the sight of Adolph Zukor ·in an unfamiliar state of excitement. It appeared, from Ferdie's account, that only a few months earlier I had come to Zukor for a job. And after several meetings with me, he had offered me a very good contract, only to find me suddenly coy and finally, after considerable vacillation, turning it down. He therefore put me down for a great fool. But the spectacular success of *Broadway* had confirmed his first judgment that I was a very smart boy. *That* of course was the reason for his excitement.

"Did you really hear that story from Mr. Zukor?"

"No, I can't say I did," said Ferdie. "I actually got it from someone in the office."

"Well, all I can say is that it is a perfect show-business story."

"You mean it isn't true?"

"I guess you might say it's true," I said, "except for maybe a few little details."

"Oh, I knew I meant to ask you something," said Ferdie as we continued our telephone conversation. "Have you read Professor Baker's biography of Hemingway?"

"No."

"Did you know that Thornton Wilder advised Hemingway not to give you his play?"

"Yes, I've heard that. I thought it was very funny considering that nothing on earth could have induced me to produce it."

"But you had just done such a beautiful production of *Our Town*."

"Well, Wilder didn't think it was beautiful. He didn't like it at all."

"I must say—of all the weird goddamn things I've heard of in show business, that is certainly the weirdest. That production has gone down in history as a masterpiece."

"I wish to hell it had made some money. I risked $44,000 on that production and never got it all back until I sold the picture rights. And then only barely."

"But after advising Hemingway not to give you his play, didn't Wilder come out to California to ask you to do *Skin of Our Teeth*?"

"Yes, he did."

"How do you explain that?"

"Why should I be asked to explain it?"

"But wasn't Wilder a great friend of yours?"

"Well, I thought so. At least until I put on *Our Town*. Eddie Goodnow's account of the opening night in Princeton is quite accurate.* In the midst of the tremendous reception the production got that night, Wilder was screeching, 'You simply don't understand my play.' Luckily for him, the applause was tumultuous enough to amount to a demonstration, so nobody but I could hear him; otherwise he might have been killed by some frenzied drama lover. Now Lee Shubert was also a friend of mine. In private life he could be very decent and considerate. But in business he could look you square in the eye and tell you a demonstrably flat lie and even offer to take an oath on it. So I enjoyed doing business with him as sheer entertainment. I have had dealings with some very rough customers, but I found it comparatively easy to get along with them. It's only when you're confronted by high-minded people like Wilder that you find yourself forced to make allowances of a particularly frustrating kind. But we must try to be fair. Wilder spent more than half a lifetime looking down at the admiring faces of students in classrooms. And in lecture halls he was looked up to by adoring middle-aged ladies, who regarded him as a sage. If hell hath no fury like a woman scorned, think of the feelings of a sage whose views on stagecraft have been ignored."

"I must say I find the whole thing rather queer," said Ferdie.

I suddenly burst out laughing. "I just recalled a story Ben Hecht once told me. As a boy of fourteen, he was taken to visit some rich relatives in New York. Now back in his home

* Edward Goodnow was the stage manager of *Our Town* who contributed an account of this incident in a book that I wrote, called *Watchman, What of the Night?.*

town in Wisconsin, Ben was considered an exceptionally bright young fellow. But here in the opulence of a huge apartment on Riverside Drive he felt lost. And he was a little miffed because none of his very rich relatives paid any attention to him. There was lively chatter going on all around him, and he was determined one way or another to break into it. With an elbow propped on the mantelpiece and an assumed expression of world-weariness, he waited for his opportunity. At last, as one of his aunts, who had been holding forth, stopped a split second to catch her breath, Ben murmured, 'I guess life is a funny proposition after all.' "

What I was really laughing at was a memory of myself on a Florida-bound plane in the spring of 1938. I was on my way to Key West to spend a few days with Ernest Hemingway, and I was in a mild state of panic.

Only two days before, his friend and agent, Mark Hanna, had sent me the manuscript of *The Fifth Column*. I read it immediately and phoned Hanna.

"Mark," I said, "if this play had come to me from a sophomore in Brooklyn College, I would have returned it with a letter of encouragement. But if the author had been a graduate student, I would have been merely polite."

"Well, I told you I thought it needs work," said Hanna defensively. He was a very odd sort of agent. He would only represent people he loved and admired, and to those lucky few he was passionately devoted. "You know I'm really worried about what you say. Don't you think you could help Ernest get it into shape?"

"I'm awfully tired, Mark." This was absolutely true. I had just opened *A Doll's House* and *Our Town* within a few weeks of each other. "And Hemingway's play needs a hell of a lot of work."

"Look, Jed. Please stay where you are. I'll call you back in fifteen minutes. I'm going to call Ernest."

I was worse than tired; I was despondent. I believed that the most terrible war in history was going to break out and that Hitler stood a good chance of winning it. And that would mean the end of the world for people like me. Outside the window of my office in the Empire Theatre, the atmosphere looked like stale bed linen, and I wished I could have liked Hemingway's play, if only to give me an excuse to go down to Florida for a few days.

As if he had been reading my thoughts, Hanna called and said that Hemingway was anxious for me to come down and that he had asked for my home number so that he could invite me himself.

"Now, Jed," said Hanna, "I know how much you admire Ernest as a writer, and I would hope you'd do everything in your power to help him."

"Tell Hemingway it isn't necessary for him to call me. Your word is good enough. Call me at ten tonight, and by that time I will have made up my mind about going to Key West."

The simple truth is that I was touched by this plea for help. I would obviously have no commitment to the play. I would simply make such suggestions as I felt he could use and feel free to go. I also secretly entertained visions of hot conch chowder, cold stone crab, and turtle steak broiled on a charcoal fire. And for a few days I would be further away from Europe and particularly from Germany.

But now, in the plane, I had reread the play and liked it even less than the first time I read it. It would not be easy to mask my distaste for it. I could be very frank about a play I had a feeling for and even brutally so when I felt it was necessary. But here other qualities were required, and I very much doubted that I possessed them. Tact is not one of my gifts.

Hemingway was cordial enough when we met at the airport. But he seemed distraught, and he looked as if he had not slept. As we drove off, he said, "Do you really think that the play needs a lot of rewriting?"

"Yes, I do."

He was silent for a moment. Then he said, "I tell you the truth—I hate rewriting."

"I don't blame you. It can be sheer drudgery. You have got to have some kind of passion for the theatre to find it endurable."

"Well, that's one passion I know I haven't got. I just don't like show business, and that goes for most of the people in it."

"I feel a little that way myself."

"Then why are you in it?"

"It happens to be something I know how to do."

"Do you really mean that?"

"I'm just about ready to quit it for good. It bores the ass off me."

Hemingway roared with laughter. "This is something of a surprise," he said. "How did you happen to get into it?"

"If I could only have gotten a job as a reporter on the *World*, I wouldn't have gone near the theatre. I finally did get a job as a reporter—but only on a theatrical trade paper. So I had to go to a lot of shows. And I thought they were almost always lousy. And it was those lousy shows that stimulated me. Because I thought I could do the thing better than most of the people in the business."

"I can understand that."

"What puzzles me is why anyone like you, who dislikes the theatre, would bother to get mixed up in it. You can sit on your duff and write anything you like and fling it over the transom, and someone is bound to pick it up and pay you a lot of money for it."

"That's a little exaggerated," he said. "But there's good sense in what you say. My wife's waiting lunch. Are you hungry?"

"Yes."

This did not sound like the Hemingway who was supposed to be so anxious to see me. I wondered if Hanna had been putting me on a little.

"Mark said you asked for my home number," I said.

"Yes. I wanted to call you personally and ask you down."

He said this so matter-of-factly that I could only make a guess that he had hoped I would make light of the rewriting and that the whole business would come off rather easily. In that case his hopes were dashed from the moment we met. But I was beginning to feel relieved and even a little exhilarated.

This mood did not last long. Pauline Hemingway, matronly

and frigid in manner, had been only too obviously waiting lunch and made no effort to conceal it. Her welcome was minimal. Hemingway introduced me to his house guest, the German novelist Gustav Regler, who had been the political commissar with the International Brigade in Spain. We sat down to lunch immediately.

The lunch began in silence and, except for a single inaudible murmur from Regler, ended the same way. A servant brought in the food, served, and then removed the plates, all in dead silence. Husband and wife never exchanged a word or even so much as a glance. I thought if anyone had struck a match the place would have blown up.

Although I had told Hanna I wanted to stay at a hotel, Hemingway astonished me by asking me to stay at his house. I thanked him and of course declined.

"I think I'm a fairly good host," I said. "But I lack the grace to be a good guest."

"I understand exactly how you feel," he said.

In a matter of minutes we were on our way to a neat little hotel five or six blocks away. I unpacked in a pleasant, spotlessly clean room and felt I was home free. I knew almost nothing of Hemingway's private life and had little or no curiosity about it. It was of course only too plain that the Hemingways were going through a very bad time. (On the way down the plane had stopped in Washington where I ran into Arthur Krock of the *Times*. He introduced me to a pretty young woman named Martha Gellhorn, who was soon to be Hemingway's third wife. But I knew nothing of these things until long afterward.) At any rate, to be out of Hemingway's house at that moment was sheer heaven.

The next morning Hemingway took me fishing. Aboard the *Pilar*, he was in his element. It was a beautiful day. The Gulf Stream was sparkling and hip deep in fish. There were sandwiches and hard-boiled eggs, gin and beer. Hemingway was jovial and even boisterous with his fisherman, and he was having a glorious time with a big club, battering the heads of the exhausted creatures as they were brought to gaff, and always saying, "*Look* at the son of a bitch. Just look at that *son of a bitch*." I enjoyed a long nap in the cabin. When I came up on deck, Hemingway handed me a drink.

"Do you think you could find somebody in New York to do the rewrite of the play? I would of course give up any share of the royalties required to do the job."

I suddenly felt deeply sorry for Hemingway. "I don't really know anyone I'd recommend. But I'm sure that Mark could find you a producer who might be helpful in a situation like this." In the event Hanna did find a producer who provided a good hack writer to do some revisions. But the result was like a cosmetic job on a cancer patient.

The following day we drove out to a lonely beach for some shooting. Thanks to a marvelous rifle with an expensive Austrian sight, I was lucky enough to hit a tin can at a distance of about 150 yards. I believe this impressed Hemingway far more than anything I had ever done in the theatre. At any rate he kept slapping me on the back and assuring me that I might have been the best sniper in Spain.

When I got back to my hotel, I found a phone message from a Miami yacht broker and, after bidding Hemingway goodbye, left for Fort Lauderdale to inspect a vessel that had come on the market. What I had enjoyed most about my visit to Key West was that I was not required to discuss the play itself. Such a discussion might have been painful for both of us.

The magazine article mentioned by Ferdie Weill turned out to be a double misnomer. It was not an article, nor was it published in a magazine. It was merely a filler in the theatre programs, and according to the writer of the filler, I had taken an option to produce *The Fifth Column* and had come all the way down to Key West to inform Hemingway that I had been unable to obtain financial backing for the production. Needless to say, Ferdie was utterly outraged by this account.

Perhaps it never occurred to the author of this fable how odd it was for a producer to go all the way down to Key West to tell Hemingway what he could have told his agent for a ten-cent telephone call. Even so, all this sounds perfectly plausible. Producers often find it difficult and sometimes impossible to raise money for their shows. What will no doubt come as startling news to the author of this squib (A. E. Hotchner), is that I had for many years been the sole financial backer of my productions and, indeed would not have it any other way. I was not unique in this respect. Arthur Hopkins, David Belasco, and Winthrop Ames, all like myself autocratic and self-sufficient, produced, directed, and financed their own productions.

Hotchner, who had obviously been useful and worshipful enough to become Hemingway's friend—a fact which he brought to public notice in a book—does not quote Hemingway but suggests that he was the source of this information. Or is Hotchner simply trying to get as much as he can out of his connection with Hemingway, even if it means inventing material for fillers in the theatrical programs? Anyway, I did not share Ferdie's fury. These are hard times, and one can view such measures with some compassion.

On the other hand, is it really possible that Hemingway should have made up such a pointless story? And if so, to what purpose? We expect politicians, businessmen, and advertising people to lie, but we are always shocked to discover that writers lie. And of course they do lie. Even so fine a writer as John Steinbeck, as his friend George Frazier has recently testified, was a fantastic liar. And so for that matter was that brilliant intellectual and great favorite of Justice Holmes, Harold Laski. Gide told the most squalid lies about a young Jewish boy in Algiers he had tried, unfortunately without success, to bugger. And even Turgenieff, whom Henry James regarded as the great gentleman of Europe, lied about some material he had pinched from Goncharov, the author of *Oblomov*.

Of course none of these artists lied like commercial people, to make money. Writers often lie out of vanity but more often out of fantasy, which is after all their chief stock in trade. Somerset Maugham, a lifelong homosexual, told Garson Kanin that the great love of his life was an actress. He was so passionately in love with her that he sailed to America, took a train to Chicago where she was then appearing, for the sole purpose of proposing to her. Her reply to the proposal was that she was pregnant by a man she was not in love with and that she was therefore compelled to decline his offer. I shall say nothing of this string of rather delicious nonsequiturs.

What seems perfectly obvious is that Maugham had been fooling around with an idea for a short story that was too feeble and Victorian for practical literary purposes. Even so, he found a way to use it.

Apart from the fact that he published the story and took money for it, Hotchner is, of course, hardly worth mentioning in such august company. I therefore refrain from characterizing him.

For that I turn back to Professor Schlesinger. He has been an ornament to the Harvard faculty, he is the author of an historical masterpiece, he occupies a chair at the City University of New York with an endowment of $100,000 a year, he has been a confidant of President Kennedy, and been close to the events in which the fate of the world may have been decided. And when he chooses to launch his thunderbolts, he selects as a target a scholar of the very first rank.

Is it fair, is it decent, to ask so distinguished a master of invective to lean forward a little and adjust his sights to a meaner level, and persuade him to tell us in good plain Anglo-Saxon English, what he would call Hotchner?

❦ OUT OF THIS NETTLE, DANGER . . . ❦

THE OPENING NIGHT OF *COQUETTE* IN ATLANTIC CITY IN
October of 1927 provided my first encounter with disaster in
the theatre. What followed was a delirious comedy in which
the chief ingredients were Helen Hayes's virginity, real or
imagined, the irreparable collapse of my relations with
George Abbott, the dissolution of my business partnership
with Crosby Gaige, a conspiracy to undermine the production
and, if possible, to abort it, the sudden appearance of a guard-
ian angel in the implausible form of a professional stage
mother and—what for me was the most distasteful ingredient
of all—the inescapable necessity to take over the production
as director. It might have been described as a comedy of
psychopaths for psychopaths.*

That what had started out as an inconsequential little comedy might generate so much sheer disruptive power would
seem as likely as a show of hard evidence that the sudden
assassination of Mao Tse-tung had been triggered by the chain
reaction from a Broadway revival of *Abie's Irish Rose.*

---

*Immediately after writing this last paragraph, I went out for a short walk.
Near Central Park I ran into Elia Kazan. Among other things I asked him if
he ever went to the theatre nowadays.

"Jesus Christ, no," he said. "I wouldn't be found dead in a theatre. When
I'm sitting at my desk in my house in the country, writing something that
really interests me, I thank God I don't have to be involved with these goddam psychopathic types that pass for actors. How's your book coming
along?"

The whole business began innocently enough in the spring of 1926 when George Abbott brought me the manuscript of a light comedy called *Norma's Affair*. When I returned it to him the next day, I said, "I find it trivial, but I'm sure somebody will produce this play, if only because it's got a charming part for Helen Hayes. But as I was reading it, I couldn't help thinking that if the heroine had to die for what began as a harmless flirtation, people would sob their hearts out for her." Abbott stared at me thoughtfully but said nothing. It was a remark that during the next year and a half I would regret a hundred times. Shortly afterward an option was taken on the play by another producer.

Within a few months that option lapsed, and Abbott told me he was sure that Ann Bridgers, the author of the play, would be amenable to an offer of collaboration which would give us a free hand to adapt the play to our own liking. I thereupon entered into an agreement with Miss Bridgers, and immediately changed the title to *Coquette*.

Turning a light comedy into a tragedy is not among the easiest things in the world to do. The remark I had made to Abbott was nothing more than a casual observation after a hasty first reading. Now I had to study the play very carefully, and I soon came to the conclusion that it would be much more difficult than I had imagined. It was not a simple problem like replacing a "happy" ending with an "unhappy" one. The whole fabric of the play would have to be ruthlessly torn apart and a drastically new balance of forces set in motion. This in turn involved subtle changes in characterization and the creation of an entirely different scale of dramatic values. It would in fact have been far easier to write an entirely new play. Yet, in the midst of a schedule that more often than not involved me in sixteen hours of work a day, I had blithely taken on a burden that frequently left me exhausted and sleepless.

Over the next year we would turn out a dozen drafts of the play, each one in turn subjected to new and often microscopic revisions. Although my literary standards were very different from Abbott's, I persisted in demanding a quality of writing far beyond his capacity. Unrealistic as this was, I was nevertheless confident I could contribute all that Abbott lacked as a writer. It would be fair to say that the undertaking was impossible, but that we somehow managed to carry it off—an accomplishment which owed as much to tenacity as to talent.

The whole matter was further complicated by the engagement of Helen Hayes for the leading role. I had regarded Miss Hayes, then a popular light comedienne, as a technically accomplished performer with an assured future in the commercial theatre as a very "cute" actress. But then she suddenly appeared in Barrie's *What Every Woman Knows*, and her subtlety and power astounded me. I decided that she was the only actress in the world to play *Coquette*. But my first meeting with her left me bemused. She seemed to have no conversation of any kind, and she did not say a word that was not unadulterated cliché. I later told Abbott that she was as ignorant as a Ubangi.

If anyone had ventured to suggest that I was even more ignorant than Miss Hayes, I would have been shocked and angry. Nevertheless I was ignorant enough to believe that it took a brilliant woman to be a brilliant actress, an error of judgment more appropriate to a hard-headed banker than to a professional man of the theatre. But of course I was still a complete amateur in show business. What was worse and certainly far less pardonable was that I was a first-class intellectual snob, and such a matter as the fact that Miss Hayes had since the age of three spent her entire life on the stage played no part in my swift and often unjust conclusions.

Intellectual snobbery was indeed one of my besetting sins. It had almost cost me the chance to produce *Broadway*. Shortly before I became a producer, I had met Philip Dunning on tour in Detroit, and over a drink he told me about his play and offered to go to his hotel and bring me a manuscript. I bluntly refused to read it. He was astonished and hurt because I would not give him any reason for my refusal. The plain truth is that I thought he was much too fatuous to write a play that would interest me, which was of course one more sign of the amateur. He subsequently sold an option on the play to William A. Brady. Almost a year later he turned up at my shared cubbyhole of an office in the Bond Building and told me that Brady's option had just run out. He laid a seedy-looking manuscript in a worn dun-colored cover on my desk and literally begged me to read it. To get rid of him, I agreed to do so and ostentatiously thrust it into a stout manila envelope already bulging with five other manuscripts. But I had no intention of keeping my word. In the event, it turned up on top of the pile when I emptied the envelope onto my night table. By eleven o'clock that night I was phoning Dunning to come to my office in the morning to sign a contract. People in the theatre often complain of being dogged by bad luck. Now I discovered that there was such a thing as being dogged by good luck. I could not help thinking that I might have begun my career with a resounding success like *Broadway*, a reflection a little too sour to be entirely palatable.

While I was producing *Coquette*, I was also working on *The Royal Family* with George S. Kaufman and Edna Ferber, as well as on a melodrama called *Spread Eagle*. This play interested me a great deal more than either of the other two. It dealt with a plot to bring about an American intervention in Mexico, a dream then dear to the hearts of mining and oil tycoons and especially of William Randolph Hearst, whose inherited millions of acres in that country had been expropriated during the Mexican revolution. Although the play did not do nearly as well as I had hoped, it was disturbing enough to induce several officials of the State Department to come to New York to study it. Unfortunately there was no Joe McCarthy around at the time to attack it as "subversive" and make a commercial success of it.

The thought has sometimes occurred to me that if I had accosted Miss Hayes at high noon in the lobby of the Waldorf-Astoria, pulled up her skirts, and raped her in full view of a crowd of goggle-eyed conventioneers, the resultant commotion might have barely exceeded the shock produced by her engagement to appear in the leading role of *Coquette*.

Chief among those who made me aware of this was my financial partner, Crosby Gaige. In the first place he did not like the play at all.

"I don't think the American public will be interested in a play about the South," he said one day.

"I don't understand why you call it a play about the South.

The plot is about a gay, well-born girl who gets knocked up by a hillbilly. Her father murders the boy, and she kills herself. I can't detect a single whiff of magnolia in the proceedings."

"I'm talking about how the public will regard the play."

"To tell the truth I don't know much about the public, and what little I do know is anything but flattering."

"The public happens to provide your bread and butter. And what the public wants ought to be your prime concern."

"I don't give a hoot in hell about the public. Anymore than the public does about me. I know what interests *me*. So I really produce for an audience of one—myself. And all I can do is hope that a few *schleppers* will somehow tag along after me."

"That's sheer arrogance and a perfect recipe for bankruptcy."

At the end of that conversation, he asked if I would mind letting him reduce his financial participation in *Coquette*. I did not mind at all, and matters were so arranged. He thus relieved himself of a profit of several hundred thousand dollars, which in time might have been enough to save *him* from bankruptcy.

Gaige did not in fact like any of the plays I was doing at the time. Before I produced *Broadway*, I was hard at work on the manuscripts of both *Coquette* and *The Royal Family*, and I offered him the same arrangements we had entered into for the production of *Broadway*. He dismissed *The Royal Family* as "too static." With what feeling he saw it sell out for a solid year in New York and ultimately turn a profit of a million dollars is anybody's guess. He even had serious reservations about *Broadway*. He thought that the "hero," a comic portrait of a feckless, cocky, small-time hoofer, beautifully played by Lee Tracy, was too conceited. The public wanted their heroes to be modest, he said. And he felt that Tracy was too obscure an actor for such an important part and urged me to get an established star to play it. When I turned down these suggestions, he complained that the trouble with me was that I would not listen to anybody. I did not dispute the charge.

Now, having reduced his equity in the venture and fully aware that I would be going into rehearsal within a few weeks, he invited me to lunch in the hope that I might be persuaded to abandon the production of *Coquette* and find some other play for Miss Hayes. He had given a copy of the manuscript to his partner in theatre operation, Edgar Selwyn, who, unlike Gaige, was really a man of the theatre with a successful background as an actor, writer, and director. Selwyn, he reported, had been deeply disturbed by the idea of Miss Hayes playing a pregnant girl in a sordid play like *Coquette*. (Later Selwyn confirmed this feeling to me. "Helen has a quality of purity on the stage," he said. "She represents something rare and fine to the public, and I honestly believe that you ought to think twice before you destroy that image forever. Incidentally, I don't think Helen can do the things she would be required to do in playing such a part.") I, on the other hand, thought she could do anything.

There were others too who were horrified at the prospect of such a profanation. Burns Mantle, an ex-typesetter who was the dramatic critic of the *Daily News*, furnished the climax to the campaign against the betrayal of Miss Hayes' reputation. One must suppose that his conscience forced him to perform an act that would be considered unethical even in the more squalid areas of the United States Senate. A week before the play was to open in New York, Mantle attended a performance in Newark and wrote a column filled with disapproval of my casting Miss Hayes in the play. But only a week later he found himself compelled to hail her performance as a great personal triumph.

In all the years I knew Charles MacArthur, I never once heard him tell of an experience in which he was the hero. It was the unique charm of this very rare broth of a fellow, who could hold his own in the roughest kind of barroom brawl, that he would invariably turn out to be the victim—misunderstood, cringing, humiliated, and defenseless. "There I stood, meek and Christlike," he would say, "with all those people throwing buckets of wet horseshit at me."

If Miss Hayes, like the girl in *The Dybbuk*, could speak with the voice of her late husband, she could tell a similar tale about the audience on her first night in Atlantic City. Having given a superlative performance and risen to her great emotional scenes with a virtuosity I have rarely witnessed, she was rewarded with outbursts of laughter. The fault lay not in Miss Hayes, nor in her stars, but in Abbott and even more particularly in myself.

During the rehearsals I had been very much disturbed by what I regarded as the excess of comedy in the first act. But Abbott thought it was delightful stuff, which indeed it was. So, against my better judgment I left these "delightful" scenes in the play. (The truth was that I had grown inattentive. My work schedule was beginning to take its toll. Before long in the midst of my rehearsals of *The Royal Family*, I would break down completely and be forced to remain in bed under medical care for an interminable week.) And there was Miss Hayes' long past as a comedienne to add weight to the audience's anticipation of a very pleasant evening of light entertainment.

Whatever Abbott's limitations as a writer, these were now reflected in his limitations as a director. The staging lacked the sensibility, the dramatic tension, and the sheer style that were necessary. (He would never again venture beyond the safer areas of slam-bang farce and musical comedy in which he finally found his true métier.)

It was with understandable mortification that I watched shocked and bewildered members of the audience emerging from the auditorium that night. Among them appeared a contingent of the top New York theatre-ticket brokers, who filed out with nothing more than polite good-nights to me. Not one of them was tactless enough to mention the play. This meant that the word would be out all over Broadway in the morning that *Coquette* was an absolute flop. And the reviews in the local press and in *Variety* would hardly add much to the morale of the company. Obviously there was a great deal to be done, and all of it was urgent. I sent word to the stage manager that I would meet the company within fifteen minutes to make some cuts.

To Abbott, who was coming into the lobby with Miss Bridgers, I said, "There are a hundred things to be done but I think we'd better begin by cutting ten or twelve minutes of that delicious comedy out of the first act."

"I don't really see any reason for panic," he said. "Why not just relax for a couple of days and give the show a chance to play itself into shape?"

I turned away from him without a word, walked into the box office, and cursed a blue streak. I finally had to tell Whitaker Ray, my manager, why I was so angry.

"If Abbott had said anything like that to me after what happened here tonight, I'd have been tempted to have thrown him out of the theatre," said Ray. "Maybe it's all for the best. Why not mark Abbott n.g. and take over yourself? You'll need time to straighten out this show. If the worst comes to the worst, you can postpone your rehearsal date for *The Royal Family*."

"No," I said. I looked at my watch and went backstage. It took me a little over an hour to make the cuts and rehearse them. I announced that there would be no rehearsal the next day except for a run-through of the cuts a half hour before curtain time. I had now been up for nineteen hours, and I would have to take the early morning train back to New York.

As a child I once heard my mother complain that I was a "boy without a limit." Now there seemed to be limits hovering over me everywhere: limits of time, limits of energy, limits of human capacity, even limits of understanding. But going over the text of the play during the past hour had somehow revitalized me. In my hotel room I sat down with the manuscript. By three thirty in the morning I had covered six quarto sheets of paper with notes for things to be altered and rerehearsed. (Before the end of the week I would have six more.) It must have been after four when I got to sleep, but I was up at seven and was able to snooze in my stateroom on the train.

In New York I got a "sympathetic" phone call from Gaige. The word had traveled faster than I had. He seemed surprised to hear that I intended to bring the play to New York. Clearly he had taken it for granted that I would abandon the project. There was other evidence that the word was harsher than I had expected. Even people on my staff spoke in hushed, guarded tones.

Meanwhile I was immersed in my casting problems with *The Royal Family*. These had now become catastrophic, and they will be explored in a later chapter.

With another nap on the three o'clock train back to Atlantic City, I was reasonably alert for the evening's performance. The effect of the cuts was definitely an improvement but not by a long shot a vital one. It was now clear to me that a long period of uninterrupted drastic rehearsal was required. There were six more performances to be given in Atlantic City, and then we were to begin an engagement on the following Monday at the Adelphi Theatre in Philadelphia. A rehearsal on Sunday would not be enough. I was almost too tired to make the short walk to my hotel. But I had my first good night's sleep in almost a week.

It was about noon when I awoke the next morning. While waiting for my breakfast in the dining room, I wrote a new scene for the end of the second act on the back of a menu. Later I had the girl in the box office type three copies of it. Miss Hayes looked at the half page of typing and said, "Ah, that's more like it." At that moment, I almost fell in love with her. As an actress, her instinct was always perfect. While we rehearsed the scene, I was called to the box office to take a long-distance phone call.

It was from Whitaker Ray back in New York. He spoke for about five minutes without interruption from me. When he had finished, I said, "You have no evidence to back up this story. And even if you did, it wouldn't do any good. Anyway, my plans are made. Please arrange to postpone our Philadelphia opening from Monday to Tuesday night. And ask Dick Maney to reserve a ballroom at the Bellevue Stratford for Sunday and Monday afternoon and evening. I won't be back in New York until late Monday night." I left the theatre and took a long walk. I had a lot to think about.

Having decided to get rid of Abbott, I found the decision painful. Though we had little in common, he was honest and hardworking. And although he was parsimonious and almost phenomenally dull, we had been friends for a long time. He always carried out my instructions to the letter, but what I suppose I appreciated most about him was that, except on a single occasion, he spared me all contact with actors. (I considered actors so feebleminded that I found it embarrassing to talk to them. In time my attitude would change, and I would even grow fond of them. It is for others to judge whether this was a sign of mellowness or the onset of premature senility.)

That one occasion arose during a rehearsal of *Love 'Em and Leave 'Em*. There was a crap-shooting scene in the play, and on the stage it had turned out to be a very dreary affair.

"George," I said, "you don't seem to know very much about crap shooting."

"No, not a thing," said Abbott. "I wish you would go up on stage and make the scene right."

I hated like the devil to do it, but it was only too obviously necessary. "Gentlemen," I said as I approached the actors who were in the scene, "whatever your sins, it is clear that not one of you can be accused of being a crapshooter. Yet it is your highest professional duty to persuade the audience that you are indeed crapshooters. You must not read lines like 'Eighter from Decatur' or 'Come on, little Joe' as if they were dry statements—they are prayers! And not genteel, polite, Episcopalian prayers but passionate, fervent prayers like those of the more fanatical Muhammadans, beseeching Allah to smite their enemies. Life and death ride on every roll of the dice."

This drew laughter, and the scene almost immediately came to life. As I started to leave the stage, Donald Meek, a member of the cast, took hold of my arm and said, "Young man, you are one hell of a director."

"Oh, no." I protested. It was not until I was halfway down the steps into the auditorium that I remembered to say thank-you to the baffled comedian. How could he be expected to understand that I just did not want to be a director?

The scene at the end of the second act of *Coquette*, as written by Abbott, reminded me of the effect on a group of people waiting tensely for an overinflated toy balloon to explode with a bang, only to see it suddenly collapse and go limp from a leak. Wild with grief over the murder of her lover, the heroine is suddenly confronted by the family lawyer who tells her that, to save the life of her father who had done the killing, she must be prepared to testify that he committed the act in order to save her honor. In Abbott's version she said, "All right, go away . . . just go away." In mine she cried, "No, I hope they hang him! I want him to die!"

I got back from my walk near the end of the second act and enjoyed seeing the new scene evoke a real burst of applause, the first applause there had ever been for the second-act curtain.

Abbott came hurrying up the aisle as the curtain fell. Miss Bridgers was with him.

"Who wrote that scene?" he asked.

"I did." I had thought he would be elated by the effect.

"You know perfectly well that you are not permitted to write anything into the play without the consent of the author."

"Well, I suppose you can always go to the Dramatists' Guild and file a protest."

"Mr. Harris," said Miss Bridgers, "I assure you that no Southern girl would say anything like that about her daddy." Then she added, "A Jewish girl might, but not a Southern girl."

"It's odd you should say that, Miss Bridgers," I said politely. "Because that happens to be the way I visualized your heroine—as a typical Southern Jewish girl. And that's why I engaged Miss Hayes to play the part."

Instead of paying me the bare courtesy of a laugh, they stalked out of the theatre. I did not see Abbott again for a long time. (Meanwhile, for the next three years, Miss Hayes went on defying the traditions of the sunny old Southland with those Jewish lines.)

After the performance I handed the stage manager a schedule of the rehearsals in Philadelphia and asked him to post it on the bulletin board. He seemed embarrassed as he read it.

"Of course I'll put it on the board, Mr. Harris," he said. "But I think Miss Hayes has made plans to see Mr. MacArthur over the weekend."

Without betraying the astonishment I felt, I said, "All you

have to do, Frank, is put it on the board. Then it becomes my problem."

"I just thought I ought to tell you, sir," he said.

"You were quite right. Is Mrs. Brown in the theatre?"

"I think she's with Miss Hayes in her dressing room."

"Ask her if it will be convenient for her to meet me in the lobby in five minutes. Tell her I won't keep her long."

"Brownie," as Mrs. Brown was affectionately known among theatre people, was Miss Hayes's mother. With her hair neatly parted in the middle and a pince-nez riding on her turned-up nose, she looked rather prim, very much as one would expect of the mother of a young woman esteemed for her purity. But she was not prim at all. She loved a joke and enjoyed good Scotch whisky. She spoke very precisely, referring to her daughter as Hel-len, not Hel'n as Americans pronounce it. I was very fond of her, not least because I once happened to overhear her say, "Now, Hel-len, you'd better listen to that boy." I was of course the boy referred to.

"Now, Brownie," I said as we sat down in the back of the darkened, empty theatre, "you may or may not know that there are all sorts of rumors afloat in New York. That Charlie MacArthur doesn't like the play, that Helen's friends who came down from Philadelphia on Monday were just shocked to see her in a play of this kind, and that she has no intention of opening in New York. Well, we both know that, contract or no contract, no actress can be compelled to perform against her will. There are always quacks available to testify, for a fee, that she is too ill to perform on the stage. Anyway, in its present condition, the play obviously isn't worth bringing to New York. But I'm sure it can be transformed into what it ought to be. So I have postponed the Philadelphia opening until Tuesday, and I have engaged space for Sunday and Monday rehearsals. I think I know exactly what must be done, and I am willing to gamble on the show as I hope it will be on Tuesday night. If I turn out to be wrong, I will close it for good at the end of the first week in Philadelphia. But to accomplish what I have in mind, Helen must be there for those rehearsals. If, however, she finds that her plans for the weekend are irreversible, I would like a letter to that effect. I will then close the show here on Saturday night and give her letter without comment or any formal complaint, to Equity." (To make herself unavailable for rehearsal during the tryout period would have been a serious breach of contract, and Equity's punishment might have been severe.)

"Hel-len," said Mrs. Brown, "will be there. Regardless of rumors, regardless of what anybody thinks or says."

"Good. I don't mind telling you that Helen does not need any more rehearsal at all. Her performance on the opening night was perfect. The production itself was like a lousy, clumsy setting for an absolutely flawless diamond. It is that setting that I shall be tampering with over the weekend."

"Well, for whatever it's worth, I want you to know I believe every word you say and that I have absolute confidence in you."

"At the moment, Brownie, it's worth a hell of a lot more than you might think."

As Mrs. Brown had promised, Miss Hayes was there all right, but I could not help wondering if she would really be *there.* My doubts almost immediately disappeared. She was more than cooperative and utterly indefatigable. By six thirty on Sunday evening we had rehearsed without interval for six and a half hours, and I had gotten through almost half the notes I had made. The company sensed almost from the start just what I was getting at, and they responded exactly the way I had hoped they would. When I dismissed them for the day, Andrew Lawlor, Jr., a brilliant juvenile actor who died young, came up to me as I was going out the door, shook my hand, and murmured, "Great, great, great." Nevertheless, I felt that I had kept them at it too long, and I was worried about how they would be feeling the next day. Six and a half hours of uninterrupted rehearsal is almost more than human flesh can endure.

By seven o'clock the next evening we were all visibly exhausted, but the job had been done, as completely and comprehensively as I knew how to do it.

"I hope you can all have your suppers in bed tonight," I said. "And stay in bed all day tomorrow. I think the show will look quite different tomorrow night, and I can't thank you

A DANCE ON THE HIGH WIRE

enough for the spirit and energy you have shown here. Good-night and good luck."

In a taxicab on the way to the Pennsylvania Station late the following afternoon, I was giving Edna Ferber a rather hilarious account of the goings-on in Atlantic City. Having gone without solid food for two days, I was feeling a bit light-headed.

"You look all wrung out," said Miss Ferber. "You look terrible."

"Ah may be black outside," I said, "but inside Ah's all white.'

"Whitaker Ray says your show's being sabotaged. What the devil does he mean by that?"

"Oh, Whit's a bit of an old woman. He shouldn't have mentioned anything like that to you. He claims he has inside information that Helen Hayes is planning to go into a new play by Charlie MacArthur and Sidney Howard—something about an evangelist called *Salvation*. It appears that MacArthur has never liked *Coquette*. Neither, for that matter, has Crosby Gaige. The opening night in Atlantic City only confirmed their opinion that *Coquette* was no good and would never get to New York. And they expect tonight's opening to repeat the disaster. If that should happen, I have already promised Helen's mother I will close the show on Saturday night. Then Helen would be free to begin rehearsals of *Salvation* under the management of Crosby Gaige."

"I am utterly mystified. How can Gaige be doing anything like that behind your back? I thought he was your financial partner."

"I had a similar impression when he agreed to finance *Broadway*. But I soon discovered that he planned a different role for himself. Being twice my age, he somehow took it for granted that fate had chosen him to be my mentor. First he asked to be billed as associate producer, although that wasn't in our agreement. Well, I don't care a hang about things like billing, so I said okay. Then he began to offer suggestions about casting, all of which I turned down. This upset him very much. And he was especially upset about my refusal to change the character of the hoofer in *Broadway*. Believe it or not, he regarded the character as too vain and immodest to be the 'hero' of a successful play."

"You're making all this up," said Miss Ferber.

"No, I'm not really clever enough to make up anything as splendidly idiotic as that. Do you know what he said when I saw him the morning after *Broadway* opened? 'Well, you got away with it!'"

"You know, all this sounds impossible to believe."

"In show business, always believe the impossible. But about the improbable, you can afford to be wary."

"Still, he seems to have impressed Helen Hayes all right."

"Oh, yes. And it's all my fault. To get him out of my hair I left it to him to draw up her contract—just to give him something to do. When I read it, I broke down laughing. The contract provides that *he* will pick out her second play. But I signed it anyway."

"Why didn't you put your foot down?"

"I'm not interested in Helen as a star but as an actress. I would have taken her even if she had been completely un-known. I don't want to be a Belasco or a Frohman, with a stable of stars to provide with vehicles. With me the play is not only the thing—it's absolutely everything. Since outside of the stage I don't know how to converse with Helen, I was rather relieved to have her do her business with Gaige. I knew she would be very much impressed with him."

"I've met Gaige and have rarely been less impressed."

"Nevertheless his clothes are cut by Wetzel, his spectacles are hexagonal in shape, his office with its marble fireplace and its shelves lined with scarlet leather slipcases is a marvel of interior decoration, suggesting scholarship, wealth, and what passes for good taste. Exactly what would impress a very conventional, inexperienced young woman like Miss Hayes."

"What does Gaige keep in those scarlet slipcases?"

"I haven't been shown more than two absolutely original typescripts of Hugh Walpole's novels and a card from Thomas Hardy formally acknowledging a birthday greeting."

"Did I hear you correctly? Did you say typescripts?"

"Yes. Gaige thinks Walpole is a major novelist, and he regards Bernard Shaw as a faker and a clown. I need only add that he writes secret 'poetry' for private publication and fancies himself a litterateur."

Miss Ferber was making a spectacle of herself, shrieking with laughter as we got into the station.

"I don't care if there is no play called *Salvation*," she said. "I don't care if Howard and MacArthur never even heard of each other. I don't care if there is no such person as Crosby Gaige. Everything you've said sounds as if Max Beerbohm somehow got himself entangled in an old E. Phillips Oppenheim plot. I hope your show is half as good as what I've heard in the last fifteen minutes."

As the six o'clock express to Philadelphia slid out of the station, we walked into the diner and were assigned a table at the end of the car. I was writing out our order when I heard what sounded like a little moan from Miss Ferber. I looked up to find her staring at something far down the car.

"Oh, no," she muttered. "This is just too much." She heaved a sigh. "Who would have suspected that I would live to revere E. Phillips Oppenheim?"

"Edna, dear, what the hell is the matter with you?"

"Do you know Howard or MacArthur?"

"I wouldn't know them if I fell over them."

"It's just as well. They're sitting at the other end of the car."

As the curtain rose on *Coquette* that night, I was cursing myself for having worked the company so hard. I could as easily have postponed the opening to Thursday night and conducted rehearsals according to a more leisurely and certainly a more humane schedule. I suddenly understood that I had been driven, even if unconsciously, by the pressure generated by all that I had heard and suspected. Now the question loomed ahead of me: Was the cast in good enough physical condition to give the kind of performance I had striven for?

Within ten minutes I knew that all would be well. Underneath all the comedy in the first act there was a tension, a tautness in the fibre of the play that had never been there before. The audience was no longer watching a comic entertainment that would turn confusingly harsh and bitter, but were almost from the first moment absorbed in a drama.

After watching the play for fifteen minutes from behind the orchestra, I walked into the box office, sank into a chair, and fell asleep. I awoke in time to see the curtain fall at the end of the second act. The applause was immense. Soon I could see Miss Ferber coming up the aisle, the bosom of her plum-colored silk dress showing dark, round stains like huge polka dots. Her eyes were red as she took my hands.

"It's a masterpiece—the whole thing," she said. "I wouldn't have believed that Helen could do anything like this."

I pointed to the tearstains on her dress and said I wished that Helen could see them.

"Don't tell me you're still worried about her. Wild horses couldn't get her out of this play. She'll get the greatest ovation since Jeanne Eagels opened here in *Rain*."

I have never seen anything quite like the ovation Miss Hayes received that night. After sixteen calls, I walked out into the lobby. The applause in the auditorium was still as strong and solid as it had been when the curtain fell. Miss Ferber appeared and hurried backstage. "If I don't get in there now, I won't be able to see her at all. Her dressing room will be mobbed."

We had fifteen minutes to make our train back to New York. I was standing on the edge of the curb, waiting for Miss Ferber, when a nice-looking man with a small mustache came up to me.

"You're Jed Harris, aren't you?" he said. "I'm Sidney Howard."

"Hello, Mr. Howard."

"I've seen you several times in theatre lobbies. I want to tell you that while this doesn't happen to be my kind of play, I think it's sure to be an enormous success."

"Naturally I prefer it that way than the other way around."

"I understand that it is very much improved over what it was like in Atlantic City."

"Well, at least the people in Philadelphia don't come to the theatre in their bathing suits."

Howard laughed. "I'd like to ask you a personal question, if you don't mind," he said. "Where do you buy your hats?" It was my turn to laugh. "Really, I mean it," said Howard, "I've always admired your hats."

"They come from Knox's on Fifth Avenue and Fortieth Street. The clerk there knows me, and I'm sure he'll be only too glad to sell you one exactly like mine."*

At this moment, Miss Ferber came out of the alley, and we hurried to the train. She was still in a state of high excitement. My memory of the return trip to New York is blurred. What I remember clearly is that she had to shake me awake in the Pennsylvania Station. I apologized, took her to her house on Central Park West, and delivered her to the elevator operator in the building. "Please take care of yourself," she said. "I don't want you to be ill. If nothing else works, think of how Crosby Gaige will be feeling tomorrow." I wasn't thinking about Crosby Gaige, about *Coquette*, about Miss Hayes, about *The Royal Family*. The taxi driver who had been waiting for me took me to my hotel. He had to shake me awake too.

---

* I ran into Howard almost two years later while walking around the reservoir in Central Park. After exchanging hellos, he said, "Say, I must tell you I went to Knox and got a hat that I'm sure is exactly like yours. But somehow it doesn't look the same on me as it does on you. Don't you think that's damned queer?"

Incidentally, *Salvation* by Charles MacArthur and Sidney Howard was produced by Gilbert Miller shortly after *Coquette* opened, with Pauline Lord in the leading role, and closed shortly afterward.

❧ A NOT SO ROYAL FAMILY ❧

MANY YEARS AGO EDOUARD BOURDET, THE FRENCH DRAMA-
tist, wrote a comedy called *Vien de Paraître*. A great success
in Paris, it was poorly produced in New York, under the title
Just Out, and was a failure. It was nevertheless distinguished
by a rare comic idea: A nondescript, utterly commonplace
young man writes a book which becomes a runaway best-
seller, wins all the literary prizes, and makes him almost
instantly rich enough to buy a fine country house where he
lives in luxury with his commonplace wife. To add to his good
fortune, the publisher loads him with huge advances on his
next three books. When a year passes without any sign of a
new book, the publisher goes down to the country to find out
what is wrong. He now discovers that the book he had published, a series of letters written by a young woman to her
husband in the trenches, was actually written by the "author's" wife. A resilient professional, the publisher turns to
the wife. She is obviously a gifted writer, so why hasn't she
gone on writing? "Ah," says her husband, "she wrote those
letters when she was lonely and unhappy. Now that we are
together and perfectly happy, there is really nothing to write
about."

Like goodness, happiness is one of the great disaster areas
of literature. Indeed if all marriages were happy, novelists
would soon go the way of farriers, coachmen, and chimney
sweeps. And comedy would of course disappear from the face
of the earth.

That is why it is difficult to write about the creation of *The
Royal Family*. If working on *Coquette* was never anything

more than hard, grinding labor, my experience with *The Royal Family* was more like a lark.

And if the original manuscript of *Coquette* had to be rewritten, the manuscript of *The Royal Family* did not quite exist. Only one act of it had been turned out when I agreed to produce it. I had run into George Kaufman on Fifth Avenue one day, and in the course of a walk back to Times Square he told me he was engaged in writing a comedy with Edna Ferber. They had just finished the first act, and he was frank enough to admit that he was not altogether sure where exactly the next two acts were going. It was evidently not going to be a conventional play with a plot, but a series of sketches of a family of actors, held together, he hoped, by a line of connective tissue which they were at the moment in the process of working out. It was obviously intended to be a kind of fond spoof on the more legendary aspects of the Barrymores. For the better part of a century the Barrymores, aristocratic in bearing and style and completely masterful on the stage, had dominated the gossip of the theatre and were thus ripe for exploitation.

The next day Kaufman sent me that first act with a brief note: "Can you see enough in this to consider a commitment to produce it?" I called him and said it gave every promise of making a lively show. A few days later I was invited to lunch by Miss Ferber.

Then in her late thirties, Miss Ferber was an immensely popular novelist and short-story writer. Since I had never met her or even seen her before, I looked forward to the encounter if only because my next-door neighbor, Alfred Lunt, had described her as resembling a magnificent Byzantine ruin. She had apparently been relieved of a rather disfiguring nose by a skilled surgeon, and the effect was altogether striking. But it was her eyes, not her altered nose, that gave distinction to her face. They were dark brown, almost black at times, and since she was incapable of dissimulation, they reflected every shade of feeling of a sensitive and generous nature. She shared a beautiful apartment with her mother, Julia, who always seemed to be off for lunch somewhere or away at a bridge party. And she possessed a jewel of a maid named

Rebecca, one of those creatures almost never seen but of whose presence and genius as a housekeeper one was always aware.

There was an awkward moment at our first meeting when I was forced to admit that I had not read any of her novels. I hastened to explain that my taste in books was rather classical and that I now found it difficult to read any fiction at all. This was, strictly speaking, not quite true. (And I was touched a few weeks later when she showed me a flattering letter from Sir James Barrie. I was of course properly "impressed." But naturally I gave no indication that I could not read Barrie either.)

Miss Ferber now sought to draw me out about the play. I was inclined to be noncommittal. Like a true disciple of Lao-tzu, the Chinese philosopher, I tried to assert nonassertion. On being pressed, however, I did venture to comment on a scene in that first act. An ex-beau of the leading lady, once an impecunious young man, returns to court her again. But now he is very rich. And he proposes to take her on a luxurious tour of the Arabian desert, with rather gaudy promises of moonlit nights in the desert, squads of camel-riding Arab servants, and a splendid caravan of richly fitted Arab tents.

"Julie has been a star for twenty-five years," I said. "And she is now well into her forties. A caravan in the desert might appeal to some idiotic 'society girl' but for a woman who has been knocking herself out in the hectic world of the theatre for a quarter of a century, rehearsing, playing, touring, with opening nights and closing nights, success and failure, and dead broke into the bargain—for a woman like that I should think peace and quiet and security would be a far more romantic prospect."

"I'm afraid you're absolutely right," said Miss Ferber thoughtfully. "I hope very much you will do our play."

Within a week I agreed to produce it. And for me the meetings I had with Kaufman and Miss Ferber were like holidays. Unlike the authors of my earlier plays, they were accomplished professional writers. Ideas for scenes, lines, jokes, and bits of stage business flew around the table while an old player piano banged out Jerome Kern's "Who" over and over again. (Miss Ferber was generous enough to inscribe my copy of the published version of the play: "For, with, and by Jed Harris." This was of course an exaggeration. I had far more to do with the writing of *Coquette*.) There was never so much as a strong difference of opinion among us, except for the old lady's death scene I had once suggested. The deeper we got into the play, the more unnecessary and even meretricious that idea seemed to me. But they were convinced from the very beginning that it was a brilliant suggestion, and they clung to it to the end. When the time came to put the show on, I tried to avoid rehearsing that death scene as long as I could—an experience I would repeat with that utterly fakey moment when Nora slams the door in Ibsen's *A Doll's House*.

Once the manuscript was completed, the fun stopped dead. Like a couple of ominous modulations in a cheerful opening movement of a symphony, auguring baleful developments to come, two shocks, administered in rapid succession, furnished the prelude to what was to become garish misadventure in casting a play.

Miss Ferber had entertained the hope that Ethel Barrymore might be induced to play Julie, the leading lady in the play. It was a hope I did not share. The part was in fact more of a presence than a role worthy of Miss Barrymore. But the ladies were old friends; Miss Barrymore had once starred in a play called *Our Mrs. McChesney*, which had been adapted from one of Miss Ferber's short stories. So I made no objection to sending the manuscript to Miss Barrymore.

The first shock was Miss Barrymore's. She regarded the play as a deliberate insult to her family and threatened us with a suit. She even consulted the criminal lawyer, Max Steuer, about enjoining us from producing the play. This, in turn, shocked Miss Ferber. And the effect of that second shock might have been even more severe if she had known that my own sympathies were not with her, but with Miss Barrymore. Long before Kaufman and Ferber had ever been heard of, the Barrymores were often referred to as the royal family of the American theatre. It was altogether natural that Ethel should have been horrified that the stereotypes passing for actors in *The Royal Family* might be identified with her own family. Ethel was nothing if not matriarchal. She had been the sole support of her father in his last long and costly illness. She had supported Lionel and his wife in Paris where he had spent a year learning to paint. And she practically forced John to go on the stage. Neither John nor Lionel had any liking for the theatre and made every effort to avoid it.

Obviously, Miss Ferber's imaginative faculties as a writer were somewhat undermined by her hunger for a star in her play. This was entirely characteristic of the playwrights who dominated the theatre in the first quarter of the century. They catered shamelessly to the whims of the stars. Even George Bernard Shaw, bereft of sexual appetites, went so far as to write passionate love letters to Ellen Terry, when all he really wanted was to get her into one of his plays.

At that time I did not even know Miss Barrymore. Indeed, we never met until more than ten years later when we were introduced as weekend guests in a Long Island summer cottage of Philip Barry's. After our hosts had gone to bed, we sat up until almost four o'clock in the morning. Ethel was then turning sixty, but she was still "opalescent," as an enraptured English dramatic critic described her in her triumphant London debut in *Captain Jinks of the Horse Marines* at the turn of the century. She had never been a great actress. Her diffident forays into "serious" acting as in *Romeo and Juliet* and Hauptmann's *Rosa Bernd* were nothing less than embarrassing. But in high comedy she had been something wonderful to behold. At once imperious and vulnerable, she made the perfect stage heroine of the time. Even when she took her bows, a picture of exquisite humility, she always lowered her eyelids with the descending stage curtain, adding an even more exquisite touch of theatrical beauty to the pleasure of the evening's performance.

Now she talked with the candor of a grande dame, and soon I was hearing an account of Alice Roosevelt's White House wedding, at which she had been one of the bridesmaids. Although the details of that highly publicized shindig are now beyond my recollection, I still remember her referring to the father of the bride, not as the President of the United States, but as "an old family friend." No doubt her children could probably refer to half the English nobility as old family friends. Ethel had of course been a great social success on both sides of the Atlantic. In London she had been courted by most of the more eligible young men in town. Not the least of those personages was the young Winston Churchill, already a highly publicized figure, with whom she had apparently not been much taken. And she was quite amused when I said that I could imagine a great comeback for him when war broke out.

"What makes you think so?" she said.

"Well, for one thing, he is an artist and a man of action. And war seems to be his natural element."

"Ah, I'm afraid you don't understand English politics. Winston was almost through after Gallipoli, and the Great Strike finished him off. Today he has almost no friends."

This was of course the accepted British view of Churchill's career at the moment. But I saw him in a different light— watching his inferiors for the better part of half a century taking the center of the stage, while he stood in the wings chewing on his own gall. His great starring role would be denied him until he was sixty-five years of age.

This nonpareil among women finished off the evening with a delightful description of John's first stage appearance in Philadelphia in a small part in one of her plays. "He hadn't learned his lines," she said, "nor did he know where he was to move during his scenes. But he was completely at ease, without even a shadow of stage fright. And the audience adored him as I knew they would. Ah, the stage was John's natural home, and how I wish he'd never left it."

All this of course lay far in the future. At the moment I was still under threat of a suit for damaging the name of the Barrymores, even as I was engaged in the task of finding an actress with the distinction of a great star to play the part of Julie. There was of course no such person. And both authors were obsessed with the idea of engaging Miss Haidee Wright, an elderly English actress, to play Fanny Cavendish, the matriarch of the family. I had seen her play Queen Elizabeth in Clemence Dane's play *Will Shakespeare*, and found myself in full agreement with George Jean Nathan who described her as looking like George M. Cohan in an ill-fitting red wig—but unfortunately without the comic genius of George M. Whatever Miss Wright was, she distinctly was not a comedienne, and she was therefore utterly wrong for the part. Nevertheless, against my far better judgment, I engaged her out of deference to their wishes.

(Almost a year later, standing with George Kaufman in the back of a packed house in the Selwyn Theatre, as we watched Miss Wright playing a scene and almost deliberately losing point after point, dawdling weirdly over her lines, I gave Kaufman a smart little whack on the shoulder and walked out of the theatre. Kaufman soon followed me. "You know you're not supposed to hit a man when he's down," he said, rubbing his shoulder. "But there's one thing nobody is going to take away from Miss Wright. For what she loses in comedy, the Chinese could live on rice for two hundred years." It is a little devastating to acknowledge that what she lost in comedy did not matter in the least. The audiences adored her—living proof, if such a thing were necessary, that the customer is not always right.)

I did not regard *Coquette* and *The Royal Family* as really good plays but as superlative shows. Unlike *Broadway, The Front Page, Dark Eyes,* and *The Heiress,* which achieved international success, these two plays never repeated their American success anywhere in the world. They were expertly contrived affairs, entirely dependent on the verve and style of their production. So, for that matter, was *The Heiress.* In its original production it was a flat failure. When I produced it all over again, a few months later, it was an instant success. But *The Heiress* could at least boast a distinguished ancestor in Henry James.

If *Coquette* owed its success to Helen Hayes' transcendent performance, it was also beautifully acted by a perfect cast. But I thought the cast I had engaged for *The Royal Family* could be described, only with the greatest charity, as adequate. And, as Max Beerbohm remarked in a review, "When we say of an actor's performance that it is adequate, what we really mean is that it is entirely inadequate."

The only member of the company who I knew would be first-rate was Charles Dickson, who was to play Oscar Wolf, the family's manager. He had given a marvelous performance as Wolfsheim, the old gambler, in George Cukor's excellent stage production of *Gatsby*. And I regarded him as the only prize in my cast.

On the day following the almost ruinous opening night of *Coquette* in Atlantic City when I returned to spend a few hours in New York, his physician called to tell me that Dickson was dying. In the context of events at that moment this news was almost shattering. He might go at any second, I was told, or he might last for weeks. As he had been kept in the dark about his condition, he was allowed to read the newspapers, and he was still looking forward to the rehearsals of the play. The result was that when I engaged Jefferson De Angelis to replace him, it had to be done in secret. A very fine old actor, De Angelis understood perfectly why it was Dickson's name that kept appearing in the listing of the cast, and not his own. Fortunately, Dickson died in his sleep totally unaware that he had been replaced or that we were already in rehearsal—a fact that we had managed to keep out of the press.

Otto Kruger, who was to play the John Barrymore role, was a good, standard, Broadway actor, entirely lacking in the distinction and elegance I thought the part required. He had been engaged because there was nobody else to be found. And I had even less hope for the performance I was likely to get from Ann Andrews in the part Miss Ferber had originally offered to Miss Barrymore.

One way and another I had delayed drawing up Miss Andrews' contract until I could arrange for Miss Ferber to see her. Miss Ann Andrews was a tall blonde with the somewhat artificial manners of a stock-company leading lady. The meeting in my office produced a heady mixture of affability (Miss Andrews') and a slight attack of nausea (Miss Ferber's). Miss Andrews sat there chatting cozily about the deplorable condition of what she called her *cunetta*, an area she discussed with the toughness of an uninhibited gynecologist. Miss Ferber was a virgin, and I tried hard to avoid her eye, but my peripheral vision was good enough to see the blood drain from her face as I undertook to steer the interview into less clinical channels.

Miss Andrews remained calm and amiable as she commiserated with Miss Ferber for turning out a play as "uncommercial" as *The Royal Family*. I doubt if Miss Ferber said anything beyond the obligatory ave and vale.

After Miss Andrews had gone, Miss Ferber sat for a long moment, rigid and stony-eyed. When she finally spoke, all she said was, "Well!"

"Oh, yes, absolutely," I said. "Can you see her actually taking Ethel's place?"

"Well, at least she looks the part."

"Yes," I said. "And so does Miss Wright."

For weeks Whitaker Ray had been begging me to postpone the rehearsals of *The Royal Family*, a campaign which he had really begun in Atlantic City.

"What you did with *Coquette* is a miracle," he said. "But you've paid a hell of a price for it. You don't sleep, you don't eat, you're beginning to look like a ghost. Your income this last month came to over $100,000, and here you are worrying yourself to death about another show with a cast that gives you the shakes. What the hell for? Kaufman and Ferber are wonderful people, and I can understand your loyalty to them. But your first loyalty should be to yourself."

Ray's figures were accurate enough. Along with *Coquette*, *Broadway* was still running in New York, and there were six companies playing to capacity all over the country.

What was difficult for me to face up to was that my vitality was at a low ebb. As a hobo I had frequently gone without food and shelter for days at a time, and I was therefore vain enough to regard myself as indestructible.

Very much against my will I permitted Ray to take me to a doctor, an altogether novel experience for me. He turned out to be a German with an office on Fifth Avenue, and I was at once fascinated by his brusque, authoritative, Prussian drill sergeant's manner. Our meeting was like an encounter between two uncongenial seals. He barked at me, and I soon found myself barking back at him. And I managed to survive a rather sadistic physical examination in which I was knocked about like a low comedian in a tumbling act.

Then, in a fresh series of barks, came diagnosis and prognosis: that my physical energy was all but depleted, and I was living on the rapidly dwindling resources of my nervous energy. And that unless I agreed to drop everything immediately, at once and forthwith, and to undertake a long rest under the strictest medical supervision, he could not be responsible for my future.

"Do you mean that if I go on working now I'm likely to shorten my life?" I said.

"Dot vood be zuh lotchical conglusion."

"I'm damned if I can understand why people want to live long. When all they can hope to wind up with is old age. Hasn't it ever occurred to you that there is such a thing as living wide?"

"Vot?"

"At my age Keats was dead, you know."

"Who?"

"Ah, I see you're not a betting man. John Keats was an honest bookmaker, God rest his soul. Doctor," I said as I rose from my chair, "I would dearly love to spend more time with you. Unfortunately I have another appointment. But please rest assured that I will weigh your opinion with all the care it deserves." Two days later I began rehearsals of *The Royal Family*.

I marveled at the way the scenes fitted together, a tribute to George Kaufman, a master of entrances and exits. Subsisting on hot tea, spiked occasionally with a shot of cognac, I reveled in the extraordinary contradictions of the play. It was, as Crosby Gaige said, "static," yet it moved with a joyous, spontaneous air which made me feel sure about the play itself and increasingly doubtful of my principal actors. It was an instance "where every prospect pleases and only man is vile"—in this case of course, one man and two ladies. "To come to rehearsal with this delicious script and find myself confronted by these 'adequate' actors," I said to Kaufman one day, "is like entering the Taj Mahal and finding a very dead *Matjes herring* on the floor."

I had engaged James Reynolds, the Irish artist and writer, to design the set, a duplex living room in a luxurious Park Avenue apartment, with a balcony and a grand staircase. As so much of the stage business involved that balcony and staircase I had the set installed in the Forty-eighth Street Theatre as a convenience to the company.

Miss Ferber was awed by the size of the setting. "It's so big," she said, "that it makes the actors look small."

"Well, they are small. When the set is properly lighted and our furniture and props are in place, the set will look much smaller. And all we'll have to do is pray that our actors look a little bigger."

On the ninth day of rehearsal, after a troubled, sleepless night, I sat in the auditorium as the cast went through its first uninterrupted run-through. All the mechanics of the production worked beautifully, but the quality of the performance reminded me of Joe Weber who, after blowing a weird, unmusical blast on his trumpet, would murmur to Lew Fields, "I can't understant it. I blow in so sveet und it comes out so sour."

There was a scene in which different members of the "royal" family were lunching, each one alone, at different small tables strewn about the stage. Fanny asks Oscar if he won't have a bit of lunch, to which Oscar replies, "Lunch is a meal I never eat." "I know," says Fanny, "just a thick soup, a chop, and a baked potato at the Astor." It was meant to be nothing more than a brief exchange of no real consequence. I had suggested to Miss Wright at least half a dozen times that the line should be spoken crisply and lightly. "I am thpeaking ath quickly ath I can," she replied. "Well, I do hope you can extend yourself just a bit, Miss Wright, if only as a personal favor to me."

Now when Oscar said, "Lunch is a meal I never eat," Miss Wright spoke as follows: "I know ... I know [there was, of course, only one 'I know' in the manuscript] h-m-m ... jutht a thick thoup ... yes, h-m-m ... and a chup ... ha ... um-n ... and a h-m-m ... baked po-ta-to ..."

At that moment I decided to fire the whole cast and start all over again sometime in the distant future. My office paid each member of the cast two weeks' salary as they were dismissed.

I was in bed in a complete state of collapse. A nurse fed, bathed, and drugged me, and my servant looked after me when she left in the evening. After two days Miss Ferber called in the late afternoon to ask how I was feeling. And then she told me she had taken the liberty of letting Winthrop Ames read the manuscript. Ames had produced a play of hers, and they were warm friends.

"He likes the play very much," she said, "and he is perfectly willing to take over the show with your cast and your production. I told him we had no idea what you planned to do. I talked to Whitaker Ray, and I gather that he wants you to postpone the production at least for a couple of months. But George and I feel that you aren't likely to find any better actors than the ones you engaged. So it would relieve us of a great burden if you can make up your mind about what you want to do."

I thanked her and told her that I was up to my neck in morphine and that I thought I could manage to come to a decision within forty-eight hours.

"I hope I don't have to tell you that we would much prefer for you to do the play," she said.

From Kaufman I did not hear a word. Working together, we had become good friends. If a good friend is someone with whom you feel free to open your heart, it would perhaps be more accurate to say that we saw a great deal of each other. He neither encouraged intimacy nor did he offer any. It was like going around with a delightful woman who happens to be incurably frigid. The first hint of his personal life came, grotesquely enough, out of one of Alexander Woollcott's more splenetic rages. He was said to have referred to the Kaufmans as "that fat Jewish whore and her withered cuckold of a husband."

If this remark left me somewhat naively incensed, it seemed to have no effect whatever on Kaufman. It was from Miss Ferber that I learned that the Kaufmans did not live together as man and wife. She had a healthy contempt for Woollcott as a monster with "clotted glands." And she urged me not to worry about Kaufman's feelings. "George doesn't really care about anything in the world," she said, "but the *New York Times*, the theatre, and bridge—and not necessarily in that order." In time I would recognize that remark as an accurate statement of fact. After a moment, she added, "You know—there's a smell of dried apples about George."

Since Kaufman knew nothing about music and painting and very little about poetry and history, conversation was sometimes difficult. The English actress Constance Collier admitted that talking with Kaufman made her very nervous. "I always feel that instead of listening to what I am saying, he is really looking for a chance to make a wisecrack." Word play, not real wit (which is a product of intellect and temperament), was his real preoccupation. And more often than not, I found it hilarious.

In that frustrating quest for good, personable actors for *The Royal Family*, even a young actor who might pass for a gentleman was hard to find. One night I went off to see an actor who had been recommended to us, and I sent Kaufman to another theatre to see a touted young player named Guido Nadzo. When I got home after a fruitless evening, I found an unsigned telegram with just two words: "Nadzo Guido."

He was neat and meticulous in every phase of his life. He even kept a little notebook in his vest pocket in which he recorded his winnings and losses at cards. And it was in connection with cards that I first observed a sign of emotion in him.

He could be very rough with waiters, but on one occasion he was quite savage. He had betrayed other signs of edginess while we were at dinner, and I finally asked him if something had gone wrong for him.

"I'm playing with real bridge experts tonight," he said. "And I guess I'm feeling a bit shaky."

"Where the hell is the fun in the prospect of an evening like that?" I said.

"Obviously," said George with a laugh, "it must be in that good old shaky feeling."

He was equally meticulous about his job as drama editor at the *Times*. Although he had an excellent staff of reporters, he called the paper between acts of a play and usually finished the evening back at his desk to scan the first edition.

And he was almost painfully meticulous about money. I had known him for almost a year when he made a small venture into intimacy by disclosing a concern about the condition of his bank account. The thought occurred to me that he might have run into a streak of bad luck at cards, a state of affairs that could be serious since (I was convinced) he counted on his winnings to augment his income. Even so I was very much puzzled. He seemed to live on a very modest scale. He had no children, not even so much as a dog or cat. He never attended a concert or the opera and, as far as I knew, he had never spent an afternoon at a ball game.

But very likely his concern about his bank account was more symbolic than real. He had just been through a humiliating failure in the theatre. He had collaborated with Herman Mankiewicz on a feeble comedy called *The Good Fellow*, an instant, total flop (produced, incidentally, by Crosby Gaige). I told him that his mistake was to have collaborated with Herman who, I felt, had absolutely no talent for the theatre. But Kaufman continued to take the failure very hard. And I suppose my own gloomy feelings about the prospects of *The Royal Family* brought him face to face with the possibility of two bad failures in a row.

He was startled when I offered him a 10-percent interest in *Coquette*, which was then about to finish its first week in Philadelphia.

"Edna tells me that it will be the biggest success of the season," he said. "What you're offering me is a gift."

"If you had a hundred dollars in the world and I needed ten dollars, wouldn't you give it to me?"

"Probably."

"Well, this so-called gift I'm offering you would be a far smaller sacrifice for me."

He shook his head. "If there were some element of a gamble and I put up my share of the money, I might go into it. But as matters stand, I just couldn't accept it."

Within a few months this meticulousness about money would take an odd turn. Just before the play was put in rehearsal, I told the authors that they might consider forgoing their royalties and sharing the profits from the show equally with me. Miss Ferber accepted at once.

"It's a very generous offer, Jed," she said. "Would we be involved in any losses we might run into?"

"No, of course not. I think I can manage the losses, if any."

Kaufman cautiously concurred in the "gamble." It was of course no gamble at all. If the play failed, there would naturally be no royalties. But in the event of success, their share of the profits would come to more than double their royalties. This is exactly what happened. My real motive for the arrangement was to provide Kaufman with a larger stake in the venture. Miss Ferber was quite rich, and she did not need the extra money.

A month or two after the play began its successful run, the manager of the show told me that Kaufman had asked to see a copy of the company's payroll. I was busy at the moment and said, "Show him anything he wants," and promptly forgot the matter. A few nights later, at dinner, Kaufman remarked that he thought I was overpaying a small-part actress in the cast.

"What the devil do you mean by that?" I said. Suddenly I remembered the incident of the payroll.

"I think she would have worked for twenty-five dollars less than she's getting."

For the first time since we met, I blew up. "George," I said, "you're supposed to be a very funny man. But you have never been funnier than you are right at this minute. Just what the hell do you care how much anybody in the company is getting?"

"It's just a matter of business," he said.

"Business! What the hell do you know about business anyway? Here you are, hauling down more than you ever got out of any three shows you were ever connected with, and now you're snooping into payrolls and settling on some poor old actress to pick on. For your information I could probably have gotten everybody in our cast for less than I'm paying them. But I don't conduct business that way. Incidentally I entered into a profit-sharing arrangement with you and Edna. But that doesn't make you my partners."

"I seem to have stirred up a hornet's nest," said Kaufman with a nervous laugh. "I just made a passing remark."

"For a clever man, George, you sound like an absolute idiot. Let's talk no more about it. You'll probably get a quarter of a million out of this play. But everything has its price. If I had paid Miss Doucet twenty-five dollars less, you might have gotten an extra five or six hundred dollars out of the show. While you're brooding about that, just remember the old saying, 'Easy come, easy go.'"

Although we continued our association and still saw a great deal of each other, I think our "friendship" was never quite the same as it had been. And I suppose he went to his grave convinced that he was right and that I had behaved outrageously.

I slept for sixteen hours and awoke the next day feeling much better. Late that morning I telephoned Winthrop Ames.

Ames had the long, thin, inbred features of a New England aristocrat. He was, as far as I knew, the chief heir to an ancient and hugely successful company that manufactured farm implements in Amesville, Massachusetts, a town founded by his ancestors. A very fine theatrical producer, he was also a solitary drinker. The first time I ever saw him, he was sitting and drinking whiskey at a table at the far end of Vincent Sardi's restaurant, then a small basement establishment where a reporter as poor as I was could afford a dish of pasta. At the other end of the place sat another solitary drinker, Arthur Hopkins. I am certain that the distance between them had nothing to do with their personal relations. It just happened that neither of them liked to talk; so their seating arrangements probably marked a mutual respect for privacy.

But for a nontalker he was rather vociferous on the opening night of his production of Gilbert and Sullivan's *Iolanthe*. I was sitting in the second row enjoying the chorus in a pretty number when I heard him distinctly calling from the wings: "Dance, you bitches, dance!"

Ames at once verified what Miss Ferber had told me. I said

I had promised to give Miss Ferber my decision the following day.

"I know. But I hope you will decide to go through with it," he said. "Obviously I'd like to do it myself, but Edna says you were of considerable help with the manuscript which, by the way, I read with great pleasure. Personally I wouldn't change a word of it. . . . I think perhaps you're inclined to underrate your powers. I had what I considered a reliable report of the opening night of *Coquette* in Atlantic City, and I never expected you to bring the play to New York. Edna filled me in on what you accomplished with two days of rehearsal. Even so I was astonished by the quality of the show. I've seen all the actors you have in *Coquette* before. And none of them ever performed as they do in that production."

"All this is heartening, I must say."

"I honestly hope so. I went over to the Forty-eighth Street Theatre to have a look at your set. It's an absolute beauty. All you really have to do is to reconcile yourself to the idea that very few of our actors have any sense of style. Most of them can't even speak decent stage English. That is a condition of life in the theatre. But I believe you can get more out of your people than anybody I know. So I hope you will go through with it."

Within the hour I phoned my office and ordered Ray to round up and reengage the company. Naturally he was shocked.

"Do you seriously mean that?"

"Yes. And arrange for rehearsals to resume tomorrow, if possible, or the next day at the latest."

"But what about you? You're supposed to stay in bed."

"Tell Davy Burton to sit in for me at the rehearsals until I can get on my feet. Be sure and tell him not to change anything I have set. All I want him to do is preside and do two run-throughs a day until I can take over again. Is the set still standing at the Forty-eighth Street Theatre?"

"Yes. Winthrop Ames had a look at it. Miss Ferber tells me he'd like to do the show."

"Yes, I know. If our bookings are still available, we can stay on our original schedule."

David Burton, a good all-around theatre man, had been engaged to act as my general stage manager. He was to maintain the quality of performances in New York and on tour.

By an extraordinary feat of energy, Ray succeeded in rounding up the company, and the rehearsals were resumed the following day. That night Burton telephoned me.

"I wouldn't have disturbed you," he said, "but I thought I ought to tell you that I saw a remarkable thing happen today. The cast was not only letter perfect but except for the fencing scene, which was a little ragged, it was more like a performance than a rehearsal. I know what you think of the cast but honestly, Jed, I think with a little luck they might get away with it."

"They surprised me at that first run-through. If they were only as talented as they are diligent . . ."

Five days later I was on my feet, still a bit rocky, and back at rehearsal. The defects in the quality of the individual performances were still blatantly there, but the performance as a whole was very different from the sum of the parts. And I was pleasantly surprised to find that my efforts during the strenuous rehearsals of the first few days had borne a few bright shoots. It also marked my discovery that perfectionism is the last refuge of the amateur, a status I was now about to lose.

The performance on the opening night in Atlantic City was as good as I could have hoped for. That the audience's response was nil did not surprise me. But the authors were clearly dismayed.

"There must be something very wrong," said Miss Ferber. Kaufman was silent and gloomy.

"What, for example, Edna?" I said. "Do you think we ought to get to work rewriting the play?"

"No, of course not. But I felt that we never captured the audience's interest."

"What sort of people do you think these audiences are? Can you imagine an intelligent person living here in the winter? This is a summer resort, with a facade of expensive beachfront hotels. Behind that facade is a frowsy, nondescript town with a nondescript population of retired clerks, letter carriers, and old folks living on pensions. When our first good comedy lines fell flat, I knew we were playing to a lot of mummies. To me it was like a dress rehearsal in an empty theatre.

"This reminds me of a story I heard about Clemenceau. There was a paralyzing railroad strike in France in 1906. When, after prolonged and fruitless negotiations, it seemed impossible to settle the strike, Clemenceau who was then the premier, ordered some of the strike leaders to be shot. For this he was bitterly attacked, particularly by the friends and supporters from his old socialist days. One of them said, 'You who were once a Communard, how could you give an order to murder Frenchmen of the working class?' Clemenceau smiled and said, 'Now I happen to be on the other side of the fence.'

"Well, I must say the same thing to you and George. I'm sure you remember that two weeks ago I fired this company. And certainly our cast isn't giving the performance we would have gotten from Ethel and Jack Barrymore and Mrs. Fiske. And this production is as different from the one I dreamed of as day and night. But tonight it came to life, a life of its own. It's not the one I hoped for, but it's real nevertheless, and I found myself caught up in it. There will be no rewriting, no cutting, no more rehearsals. And if such a thing were possible, I would be willing to open tomorrow night in New York."

"I must say it's very encouraging to hear you talk like that," said Miss Ferber. "If only the audience—"

"They won't improve. Tonight I think you had the elite of Atlantic City in the house. They will only get worse. But on Saturday night we will get an audience from Philadelphia and New York, people who've heard of the Lambs Club."

"There was something of your own warmth in the performance tonight, Jed. I felt that very strongly. I suppose that's the reason I was so stunned by the audience's reaction."

"After the first few moments, I completely forgot the audience. I don't have to tell you that I am a much tougher audience than anybody in that house tonight. And when I tell you that I was delighted and even touched by the show, you surely must believe me."

The box-office reports for Saturday night were very good. At least we would have the kind of audience the play needed—knowledgeable, sophisticated, and show-wise. And the spirits of the authors, after a great deal of buffeting, would at last be lifted. So I looked forward to the performance that night.

I was pleased to see some of the early arrivals in dinner jackets and evening dress. It was true that there were signs here and there of overfeeding, both visible and audible, and there was an unmistakable aroma of bootleg liquor. And there was a little epidemic of belching, discreetly muffled of course, and some coughing, but it was after all the middle of December, and it was a cold, damp night. It was obvious that the major part of the audience would be late so we held the curtain as long as we could.

My attention was directed at a portly, middle-aged couple who arrived as the house lights were being dimmed. They were gallantly supporting each other as the usher led them down the aisle to their seats. The footlights were glowing as the gentleman sank heavily into his chair. As the curtain rose, his eyelids descended, and they remained closed during the entire first act.

Between the endless stream of stragglers and the burpers, all backed by what seemed like a well-rehearsed chorus of coughers, the first fifteen minutes of the play were torn to shreds. I saw Miss Ferber's face, floating over the railing behind the orchestra, and I thought she would never again believe anything I said.

Between the first and second acts, I ran into Kaufman who was prowling around for samples of comment. He moved through clusters of people like a long, lean, Jewish Hawkshaw, his head cocked as if favoring a stiff neck.

"Did you hear that tremendous fart in the lobby just as the curtain was going up?" he said when we met.

"You mean there was evidence of an eructation in the foyer?"

"That was no goddamn eructation. I ought to know a legitimate fart when I hear one. And it occurred as the ticket taker was handing the man his stubs."

"I think it was damned decent of him to relieve himself before entering the auditorium. What are they saying?"

"Do you know," said Kaufman with something like wonder, "I haven't heard a single remark about the play."

"Ah, you see, George? I told you we'd have a much more intelligent audience on Saturday night."

I had apparently terminated my enforced rest too soon, and on the opening night in New York I was back in bed. And my bags were packed for a trip to Florida on the next morning. At about a quarter of eight, Miss Ferber turned up in a beautiful peach-colored dress to bid me good-bye before going to the theatre. My servant brought some champagne, and amid the toasts she said some nice things I was grateful to hear.

"How do you think it will go tonight?" she said.

"Like a house on fire. Within fifteen minutes after the first rise of the curtain, the audience will know that they are in for one hell of an evening."

"I don't know what to expect but I put all my faith in your instinct."

We sipped a little more champagne. She made a lovely picture in her pretty dress, and there was a flash of scarlet from the lining of her fur coat which lay on a wing chair beside her.

"Edna," I said, "what with *The Royal Family* and *Showboat*, this is going to be remembered as the Ferber season . . . and you really deserve everything you're going to get out of it. You've stood up beautifully in trying circumstances, and I must tell you you're a credit to the human race."

"Ah, that's nice to hear," she said. "Now that it's all over with, I wish we had agreed for you to take a month off before going into rehearsal. We really pressed you too hard. Thank God you're off to Florida tomorrow. I'm sure the sun will do you a lot of good."

We were chatting pleasantly and sipping champagne when

she looked at her watch and gave a little shriek. It was ten thirty.

"Oh, I've missed the opening," she cried mournfully. "I can't believe it. Jed, please check the time. Something may have gone wrong with my watch."

Without a word I swung the little clock on my bedside table around. She stared at it and murmured, "Oh, dear, I'm so upset."

"So am I. I wouldn't have had you miss this for anything in the world. You could either leave now—and I'm sure you'll still be able to see the company taking their calls—or stay here for another ten minutes, and then Dick Maney will call and give us all the dope."

"Oh, dear," she said distractedly. "I think I'll wait. Can we have a little more champagne?"

We had finished a demi and another was brought in. As we raised glasses to each other, the telephone rang.

"Sire!" It was Maney's voice, and the salutation was a sign that he was drunk. "I have the honor to bring you homage and intelligence from Marshal Ney himself. The enemy is routed and in full retreat. My left wing crumbles, my right wing falls back. With my unguarded center I attack. *Attaquez, mes enfants, attaquez! Toujours attaquez!*"

"Sober up, my faithful paladin," I said, "and pass your intelligence on to Miss Ferber who is sitting here beside me."

"Sire, I'm almost certain I just saw her in the lobby."

"That's her double, Dick. You know—assassins." I handed the phone to Miss Ferber. Her face was soon wreathed in smiles as Maney began describing the opening night.

"Ah, how wonderful," she said blissfully. And she kept murmuring, very softly, "Oh, not really! . . . How perfectly marvelous! . . . Oh, no, I can hardly believe it! . . ."

❧ HONDLING* ❧

I HAVE SAID ELSEWHERE THAT I NEVER REGARDED THE theatre as a business. But of course it is not called show business for nothing. It is a business, and like most businesses it is grotesquely inefficient, beset on one side by greedy real-estate operators and on the other by even more greedy unions, proliferating like maggots on a decaying corpse.

If I detested business, I detested trading even more. Or at least I thought I did. I was somewhat horrified to discover that there were times when I could find it amusing and even enjoyable.

Such an occasion arose very late one night in January in 1929. I was fast asleep when my telephone bell rang.

"Hello," said an unfamiliar voice. "Is this Jed Harris?"

"Yes."

"This is Ha'w'd Hughes."

"Hello, Mr. Hughes. What can I do for you?"

"Oh, nothin' in particular," said Hughes in a Texas drawl. This was obviously a little fib, a somewhat infantile opening gambit in what I was sure would be a trading comedy. Indeed I was not altogether surprised to hear from Hughes. "How's business these days?"

"Just about the same as it always is. The hits are prospering. The failures are not."

"Say, tell me, is there any show in New York that would make a good vehicle for a female movie star?"

---

* A show-business term derived from the German, which means doing business.

"I don't know what you mean by a female movie star. Is she a young girl or a mature woman?"

"Well, let's just say an established woman star. Can you think of any show that I ought to look into?"

"No, I'm afraid I can't."

I suspected that the woman star was Billie Dove, with whom he was reported to be involved.

"You got some kind of a show about the newspaper business runnin' now?" said Hughes after a moment of silence. This vague, almost absentminded allusion to one of the biggest hits of the year almost made me laugh.

"You wouldn't by any chance be referring to *The Front Page*?"

"Yeah, that's the one. The name just slipped my mind." It was extremely unlikely that *The Front Page* could have slipped anyone's mind, but of course it would have been impolite to say so. "Are the picture rights for sale?"

"Yes, they are."

"Well now, supposin' I was to offer $50,000 for the rights— what would you say to that?"

"Absolutely nothing, Mr. Hughes."

"What do you mean by that?"

"You merely made an ambiguous, highly conditional suggestion. Are you actually offering $50,000 for the rights?"

"Yes. That's what I meant."

"In that case, I will tell the authors of your offer. As you are probably aware, we own the film rights jointly. Naturally, they have as much say-so as I do."

"Will you let me know what they say?"

"Well, if what they have to say is in any way encouraging, I will certainly get in touch with you."

I knew that Ben Hecht and Charles MacArthur would leap at the offer. They were very much exasperated because during the eight months *The Front Page* had been the reigning success of the season, there had never been the slightest sign of a film offer. I myself was only barely less exasperated.

But the explanation was fairly simple. The picture companies were at the moment in an advanced state of disarray. The first "talkies" were beginning to appear on the horizon.

And at a time when movies were still formally censored by the office of an Indiana politician named Will H. Hays and, more subtly, by the Roman Catholic Church, the novel element of spoken dialogue presented terrifying problems. What would the censorship permit one to say from the screen? And not say? The films were now being drawn closer to the more liberal atmosphere of the theatre—a dangerous world whose denizens could blithely tell the priests to go to hell.

And, difficult as it is to believe, the innocent theatrical frolic known as *The Front Page* was considered an outspoken and even "dirty" play. One of the Gershwin songs of the period has a line:

"Language that would embarrass
Jed Harris."

But I had heard that the director Lewis Milestone had gone wild over the play. And he had done a funny picture comedy called *Two Arabian Knights* for Hughes, one of the very few successful films Hughes would ever be associated with. Obviously, Milestone's was the spur that had set off this bizarre young Texan. That is why I was not very much surprised to get the call from Howard Hughes.

"Grab it!" said Hecht when I told him of the offer on the following morning.

"I don't intend to do anything of the sort, Ben," I said. I then went on to give my reasons for ignoring Hughes' offer. I made out a good case for my strategy. A more detached witness might have described it as a brilliant case. But to no avail. Hecht launched into a passionate denunciation of Hollywood: how they blew hot and cold out there; how, one minute they were ready to offer you the earth for a story and then suddenly lost interest in it. We had spent months waiting for an offer. Now the offer had come. The moment had to be seized because by tomorrow it might evaporate. MacArthur just sat there in my office, pulling on a lock of his hair and looking rather sleepy.

Hecht and I never seemed to agree on anything. We got off on the wrong foot from the very beginning. We were introduced by the writer Konrad Bercovici. We laughed at each other's jokes, and soon Hecht was telling me of a play he had

A DANCE ON THE HIGH WIRE

written about a character named Dmitri whom he described as a sexual fireman. We made an appointment to meet in front of the theatre the next night. I waited from eight o'clock until nine thirty, but Hecht failed to show up. I figured he had forgotten the appointment or that he had been taken sick, and thought no more about it. But it turned out that Hecht had been waiting in front of the Selwyn Theatre where my production of *The Royal Family* was playing while I was waiting in front of the Broadhurst, the home of *Broadway*, which had become a sort of hangout for me. Hecht would not accept my explanation. He accused me of deliberately standing him up, and he gave the comedy about the sexual fireman to Al Lewis and Max Gordon, who were forced to abandon it in some town in Pennsylvania.

Yet, despite my seeming breach of good manners, he brought me the manuscript of *The Front Page.* I was scheduled to go to Boston that afternoon, and I promised to read the play on the train. We arranged to meet the following day.

The next morning the faces of Hecht and MacArthur were radiant with smiles as I gave them an account of the near-scandal I had caused in the club car of the Boston express by my frequent howls of laughter as I read the manuscript. My fellow passengers were first disturbed and then infuriated as I exploded from time to time. All they could see was a young man with a long nose buried in a mass of typewritten sheets which more often than not fell in untidy heaps on the floor around him as he succumbed to uncontrollable convulsions of laughter.

Now, without even pausing for breath, I said, "We are going to have a really great show. All we have to do is throw out the second and third acts and start from the end of the first act—"

"Give me that goddamn script," said Ben. He stood up and reached across my desk for it. "I heard you were a son of a bitch. Now I know it."

He walked out of my office with MacArthur in close pursuit. I was naive enough to be astonished by Hecht's behavior. I did not realize that I was, for the first time, involved with a "literary" man. Hecht had made his mark as a superlative reporter, then as a novelist and short-story writer. A different breed entirely from the likes of George Abbott and George S. Kaufman, stage craftsmen with whom I had thus far done almost all my work in the theatre. Unlike Edna Ferber who was a far more successful writer, Hecht was very much conscious of himself as a literary figure. His first novel, *Erik Dorn* (1921), had been taken very seriously by the critics. And *Count Bruga* (1926), his lampoon of a fellow writer, had been hailed as a comic masterpiece.

I was even more astonished a few minutes later when MacArthur half-dragged and half-carried Hecht back into my office.

"At least," said Charlie, "let's hear what the son of a bitch has got to say."

"Sit down, gentlemen," I said. "I'm sorry I offended you, Bennie. I suppose I should have begun by telling you that there isn't a page in the manuscript that isn't terribly funny. But a play isn't just a collection of funny scenes. What you have now is like a clock with the minute hand moving steadily while the hour hand never moves at all. There is only a single line of action that I can see holding the play together, and that is the effort of Hildy Johnson to get out of the newspaper business. At the end of the first act he is temporarily held up by Earl Williams' escape. At the end of Act II he is again held up by Molly Malloy's jumping out of the window. And at the end of Act III, having finally gotten on the train to New York with his prospective bride and mother-in-law, he is going to be brought back by some crooked device we will invent. And this will provide us with the theme of our show—once you get caught in the lousy newspaper business you can never get out again."

I then went on for another ten minutes, indicating the incidents and construction of the play as I saw it.

There was a big smile on MacArthur's face as he turned to Hecht. "Well," said Ben. "I still say he's a son of a bitch. What is embarrassing is that I have to admit he's a son of a bitch with genius."

With the help of George Kaufman, who supervised the construction of the play (and also provided the title), the writing was finished within a couple of weeks, and we had all become good friends.

But then a new row broke out between Ben and me about my casting of Lee Tracy for the part of Hildy Johnson. Hecht simply could not see the actor who played the little hoofer in *Broadway* playing a role described in the manuscript as a "big, pants-kicking Swede." I said I didn't feel obliged to reproduce the actual physical types of the original characters. (It was one of the marvels of *The Front Page* that although all the characters were actual people, nobody ever thought of sueing us for invasion of privacy. Indeed they all turned up for the opening night in Chicago and simply wallowed in delight. When the curtain fell at the end of the first act, the roar that rose from the auditorium sounded like the bellowing of a herd of wild animals panicked by a fire in a zoo. Above this din one great monster of a voice could be heard yelling: "MAKE IT MORE PERSONAL!") But Tracy was of course magnificent, and Ben, somewhat mystified by the queer business of acting, finally acknowledged that Tracy was very fine.

"Now, if you don't want to sell," said Ben, having concluded his anti-Hollywood tirade, "you can give us your check for our share of the $50,000. And you can go on playing your little game with Howard Hughes."

"Okay," I said. "Hughie Schaff will be back here in a few minutes and draw the check."

"Don't draw any check for me," said MacArthur. "Ben," he said, turning to Hecht, "I think I'll string along with Jed."

If I was surprised by this turn of events, Hecht was really astounded and hurt. They were such close friends that, even today, I cannot think of them apart from each other. Hecht gave MacArthur such a look as Damon might have given Pythias if he had caught him in bed with some other lovely boy. Even I was a bit flabbergasted. MacArthur was considered a cautious man with a dollar, and here he was, like a saint turned profligate, backing a confirmed gambler like myself. The denouement of this minidrama was even more unexpected.

"Okay, Charlie," said Ben mildly. "If that's the way you feel, I'll go along."

Over the next two weeks I must have gotten half a dozen phone calls from Hecht. These grew less jocular in tone as I was compelled to say no each time I was asked if I had heard from Hughes. In the last of these calls, he said, "Don't you think you ought to give Hughes a ring?" "No," I said. "Any call I might make could only mean capitulation. I've made my bets, and I have to stick with them."

The next night I heard from Hughes. His tone was plaintive. "I thought you were going to call me," he said. "I don't know where you got that idea," I replied, "I said I'd call you if I had any encouragement from Hecht and MacArthur."

"What did they say?"

"I don't remember their exact words. They were definitely unresponsive."

"How much do those bastards want, anyway?" said Hughes irritably.

"I haven't the faintest idea, Mr. Hughes," I said. Lying, once you got into the swing of it, seemed to come easier and easier. Then, on impulse, I inserted a delicate probe into these murky waters. "By the way, if I were you I wouldn't let it get about that you referred to MacArthur as a bastard. His people are from Kentucky, and he would take any reflection on his mother as a deadly insult. He also happens to be a very powerful fellow, and once he's aroused he is capable of great violence."

"Naturally I wasn't talking for publication," said Hughes. "It's just one of those remarks people make in workin' out a deal. I'm now gonna make my last and final offer: $75,000. Will you let me know what they say?"

"If you don't hear from me within forty-eight hours, you may assume that your offer isn't acceptable."

Now I made a tactical error. I told Ben and Charlie of the new offer. Hecht was of course all for settling the business right then and there. Again I offered to give them my check—this time for $37,500.

"If I should get more than $75,000, Bennie," I said, "it will give you a wonderful opportunity to tell people how two innocent schnooks like you and Charlie were conned into selling out by a cold-blood exploiter of talent like Jed Harris."

. MacArthur seemed to be wavering. "What do you really think, Jed?" he said.

"Well," I said, "there's been so much lying between Hughes and myself that the only thing I'm afraid of is that I might bust out laughing in one of these phone conversations and queer the whole pitch. Short of that, I think we'll get more money." Then I told him of my invention of his Southern background. This helped restore the spirit of gaiety that usually prevailed whenever we got together.

"My mind supports you, Jed," said Ben. "But, goddammit, my heart palpitates."

Within a week Hughes raised his last last, final, final offer to $100,000.

I now took a position which was not merely immoral but illegal as well. I decided not to tell my partners of this new offer. Instead I wrote out a check for $50,000, made out to Ben Hecht and Charles MacArthur, put it in an envelope and gave it to my general manager, Whitaker Ray, and instructed him to give it to them if the negotiations with Hughes broke down. Ray was shocked.

"They're not entitled to this money," he said. "They've been willing to gamble with you. Why shouldn't they take their chances the same as you?"

"In the first place, they haven't been entirely willing to gamble at all. They've been persuaded to go along with me. In the second place I'm not even telling them of this new offer, because they'd raise holy hell if I didn't accept it. And I don't want to accept it, because I'm almost dead sure we can get more."

"Then why bother to write this check and ask me to hold it?"

"Because there's always a chance that something will go wrong. Hughes might grow tired of this protracted negotiation or he might be distracted in favor of some other property. I'm taking a risk in not telling them we have an offer of $100,000. But since they don't know what I know, they shouldn't be obliged to share that risk. Anyway, Whit, that's the way I want to play it. So will you please do what I have asked?"

"If you ask my opinion," said Ray, "you're playing this too fine. A hundred thousand dollars is a lot of money. Why not make it easy for everyone concerned and accept the offer?"

"I'm like somebody who hates gambling casinos, but when the dice are handed to him, he rolls for two dollars and wins. As he is anxious to get away from the table, he lets the four dollars ride and wins again. Then he rolls for the eight, the sixteen, the thirty-two, the sixty-four, and the whole $128. When he wins that bet, he finally draws down $156 and starts betting a hundred a roll. In other words, he is hooked."

"And he'll go broke before the night is out."

"Very likely. Meanwhile I've gotten so goddamned fascinated with the game that I have to watch myself to keep from believing my own lies."

"Oh, what a tangled web we weave," quoted Ray, "when first we practice to deceive!"

Like most gestures, this one was futile too. Within a week Hughes had raised his bid to $125,000. And I accepted it. Of course Hecht and MacArthur knew nothing of this. They still supposed we were bogged down in a $75,000 heist, and they were, like expectant mothers, in a highly nervous condition. As I did not trust myself to talk to them personally, I had Ray ask them to join me for lunch the following day. I wanted to make something of an occasion of my disclosure, so I had Henri, the headwaiter in the Hunt Room of the old Astor Hotel, prepare the prized corner table with a bowl of fresh flowers. Over the drinks and caviar, in response to the now feverish curiosity of my guests, I finally let myself be persuaded to announce the long-awaited results of my exhausting pas de deux with Howard Hughes. I said I had agreed to accept $100,000 for the picture rights to the play.

I need not dwell on the rejoicing that went on over the delicious lunch, backed up by a couple of bottles, furnished by an accomplished bootlegger. Ben awarded me the palm as a master of flim-flam. I modestly described my feat as a mere finger exercise for what I hoped would be a great career as an international crook.

Over the brandy and cigars, flavorsome Upmann Penatellos, Number 34 Double Claro, I thought we looked like three bloated swindlers. It was then that I announced that I had perpetrated a fraud. "I didn't want to spoil your lunch," I said, "but we're not going to get $100,000." Their faces, gleaming and rosy in the reflected light from their brandy glasses, were a study in bewilderment. "The price is $125,000." And then, for the first time, I filled them in on all the details of the negotiations. There was naturally a good deal of laughter and backslapping. The glasses were refilled.

Hecht took a long swallow and gazed thoughtfully at his cigar.

"I wonder," he said, "if we couldn't have gotten $150,000."

"Jesus Christ, Ben," MacArthur yelled across the table. "Let there be an end to this goddamn thing."

And so it ended, the whole preposterous farrago of lies, postures, last offers, final offers, threats of violence, and midnight telephone calls. But I have not the slightest doubt in the world that I could have gotten $150,000.

❧ LIKE A FAIRY TALE ❧

For those suffering from a compulsion to read all the news fit to print, the tidings on the front page of the *New York Times* on the morning of April 16, 1930, were no more drab than usual. A group of Manhattan tenants had denounced their landlords as bandits and robbers. White persons were being attacked in broad daylight on the streets of Asia—not in Peking but in Calcutta. Comparatively refreshing was a statement issued by Mr. Hoover. The President announced that America was in urgent need of intelligent leaders, a view shared by most of the readership. Unfortunately they were for two long years powerless to act upon it.

The more fastidious reader barely glanced at these trifling items and turned rapidly to the drama section. There the news was somewhat brighter.

"After a year's absence from Broadway," wrote Brooks Atkinson, then a mere reviewer, not yet sanctified in the manner of the late Billy Rose and Mark Hellinger, "Jed Harris has returned to stage a luminously beautiful performance of *Uncle Vanya* ... and to reawaken an old confidence in his uncanny perceptions. Producing Chekhov requires more than anything else the ability to translate limpness into limpidity and to see high comedy where most observers see merely the gloom of futility. With a cast including such variegated talents as Lillian Gish, Walter Connolly, Osgood Perkins, Joanna Roos, Kate Mayhew, Eugene Powers, and Eduardo Ciannelli, Mr. Harris has succeeded brilliantly. The simple generalities of a genius emerge as detached wisdom and beauty leavened with the humor of compassion."

Mr. Gilbert Seldes' remarks in the *Graphic* were more succinct. "With superb judgment and great tact, Jed Harris has made his reentry into the American Theatre. It is a great thing for the theatre that the most exciting and interesting man in it should return so handsomely."

The only reviewer who was a dramatic critic by profession, rather than through the absentmindedness of some forgotten newspaper editor, stated flatly: "Jed Harris' presentation of Chekhov's *Uncle Vanya* is the most intelligent and by all odds the most completely satisfactory production of a Russian play that the English-speaking stage has known in the many years I have been criticizing it." There were good reasons beyond any actual merits of this production why Mr. George Jean Nathan happened to find it so particularly satisfying.

After spending the better part of a year in Europe, I had come back to New York in January of 1930. When I had closed my office early the previous spring, I was sure I had finished with show business forever. I had never regarded the theatre as a profession or even a business, but as an adventure. And the end of an adventure is like a love affair that is over; it may be resumed but it cannot really be revived. One knows these simple lessons, yet ignores them in practice.

What had happened between my departure and my return was, of course, the stock-market crash, which severed the twenties from the thirties with the efficiency of a guillotine. Though not quite decapitated, I did bleed.

In the manner of a sleepwalker, following a rather drowsy lunch with Lee Shubert, I had somehow acquired a suite of offices on top of the Morosco Theatre and awakened to find myself in possession of a staff and a payroll. It was obviously vital to do something about this. But for several weeks I had been immersed in the text of *The Cherry Orchard*, and all I could think of was how magnificent Laurette Taylor might be in the role of Madame Ranevski. For anyone seriously bent on restoring his fortunes, this was probably not a practical way to think. There are easier ways to get rich than by producing Chekhov. And to add to the unworldliness of the prospect, Miss Taylor was an alcoholic. Yet I was sufficiently tempted to ask her to come to my office.

She arrived in a state of high excitement, not, as I must hasten to make clear, because I had asked her to come and see me, but because of a play, a poetic play, she was in the midst of writing. She was buttoned up to the neck in a long, somewhat tattery fur coat, and, as though hiding a shabby dress or perhaps no dress at all, she kept it buttoned during the half hour she spent with me. She recited long passages from her play, evidently a monologue for a woman incapable of love; and she made a lovely gesture of opening a hinged door over her breast and bringing out not a heart, but a piece of cardboard.

It was a fateful gesture. Not long before, Gilbert Miller had fired her from the cast of a play called *Her Cardboard Lover* and replaced her with another actress of genius, Jeanne Eagels. If the lines which rose from her lips were not particularly distinguished, Miss Taylor herself seemed like sheer poetry. She was radiantly happy to find me a good listener and promised to send me the manuscript as soon as it was finished. The subject of *The Cherry Orchard* and Madame Ranevski never actually came up. Indeed, in the euphoria of that occasion, it might have seemed inappropriate if not entirely irrelevant.

I have never ceased to regret that I did not make a more determined effort to produce *The Cherry Orchard* with Miss Taylor. It would have been a great gamble, but it was the sort of chance I was meant to take. She had wasted her best years in two long-running popular successes, but she was born for better things. Almost fifteen years later she brought *The Glass Menagerie* to life as no other actress has ever succeeded in doing. But even before that, I had gone to see her in James Barrie's *The Old Lady Shows Her Medals*, and found myself so torn by her performance that, in an effort to get control of my feelings, I hurried out into the alley of the Belmont Theatre as the curtain fell. After a few minutes, I walked out into Forty-eighth Street, only to run into the house manager.

"Mr. Harris," he said, "what happened to you? I've been looking for you everywhere."

"Why?"

"I wanted to tell you about Miss Taylor. I'm terribly sorry you had to see the show tonight."

"What the devil are you talking about?"

"Didn't you notice she was sitting down all during the performance?"

"I didn't notice anything except that tonight she was probably the greatest actress in the world."

"Honest to God, do you really mean that, Mr. Harris?" he said. "We weren't even sure we would raise the curtain tonight. She couldn't even take a step, she was so drunk. That's why we had to put her in a chair."

A few minutes after Miss Taylor left, Osgood Perkins dropped into my office.

"People tell me that you are a genius of the theatre," he said. His tone was deadly, like a challenge to a duel.

"No argument here."

"*The* genius of the theatre."

"Well, we needn't haggle."

He whipped out a hard-used silver cigarette case, lit-up and blew an immense cloud of smoke in my direction.

"Then why the hell can't you find a nice little comedy with a decent part for me?" He now raised his voice in a parody of a Southern politician launching his peroration. "And I say damn and double damn Patrick Henry. Actors are the only people in the world who understand the perils of liberty. And they want no part of it. Have I made it sufficiently plain that a little salary would be damned useful right now?"

"Are you broke?"

"No, but I think I will be if you don't come up with something."

I could not help reflecting that people like Perkins, who had gotten little enough out of the stock-market boom, would not be spared the consequences of its collapse. As his name would suggest, Perkins was a Bostonian and by no means an improper one. Besides being exact contemporaries in the theatre, we were friends, and I hated to think that he was troubled about money. Like other fine actors, he had absolutely no judgment of plays or even of parts. He had actually turned down the role of Walter Burns in *The Front Page*. "Please don't ask me to play it, old man," he said. "I'm absolutely wrong for it. And I would only louse up your show." It took all my powers of persuasion to get him to come to the first rehearsal. His performance was, of course, a masterpiece of comic acting, a triumph he was never to equal.

"What are these?" he said. He had picked up a book from a little stack on my desk.

"If you've read one, you've read them all."

"*The Collected Plays of Anton Chekhov.* Damned depressing stuff, isn't it?"

"Chekhov will be amused to hear you say that."

"He's dead, isn't he?"

"At the moment, he's looking down from Heaven and laughing at you."

My phone rang. I picked it up and said, "Oh, by all means have him come in."

"Who is it?" said Perkins.

"A competitor."

The door opened, and Walter Connolly came in. The two men embraced each other with a warmth which, among actors, signifies just so much sound and fury.

"You will please note, Walter, that I got here first," said Perkins.

"I have no objection to standing in line," said Connolly with some formality. "I merely came to explore the prospects for a little walking-around money."

"This is beginning to sound like the streets of Cairo," I said. I had known Connolly even longer than Perkins. At the moment, I found myself studying his face as if I had never seen him before. I thought that age and suffering, perhaps, had given a nobler cast to his features. On the other hand, it might have been a run of bad luck at the racetrack. "There are few spectacles as depressing as a brace of actors screaming for baksheesh. For any silver you hope to get around here, you will have to render services. For openers, I suggest you each take a copy of this book and spend an evening of self-improvement by reading *Uncle Vanya!*"

"Chekhov?" said Connolly doubtfully. "At this time of the year?"

"Can you imagine anyone cruel enough to expose two indigent hams to Chekhov for a joke?"

"But, Jed, is there any chance you can get it on this spring?"

"If you'll both join me for lunch at the Astor tomorrow, all will be revealed."

"What parts are we reading for?" said Connolly.

"All of them. For once, try to forget the habits of your wretched profession and read the play like scholars and gentlemen. I will of course guarantee you against personal injury."

Before the afternoon was over, I had telephoned Lillian Gish, Rose Caylor (Mrs. Ben Hecht), Jo Mielziner, Fania Mindell, the costume designer, and Jane Broder, the most intelligent of all actors' agents and for many years my unofficial casting director. And I spent the evening in Nyack discussing with Miss Caylor the new translation she was to make of *Uncle Vanya*. Barely three weeks later, the play was in rehearsal.

When I said I had been immersed in *The Cherry Orchard*, it was probably in the spirit of the nurse who walked into the physicians' private dining room in the most expensive hospital in New York and reported that her patient insisted on having borscht for lunch. The doctor in charge, who was sluicing down his own lunch with a glass of wine, sighed. In the humane language of modern healing, the patient had been for almost six months a "terminal case." And though he was somewhat ornery about his diet, he could well afford the enormous fees he was paying. So he was kept alive by hook and (in the opinion of other doctors, unfortunately unfee'd) by crook. "It will very likely kill him," said the doctor, "but I guess you'd better let him have it." It was a painful and expensive accommodation. He had gotten enough out of the patient for a substantial down payment on a charming country house in Connecticut, and he had hoped the fellow would last long enough to pay for an extra bathroom his wife had been nagging him about. In the event, his prognosis was faultless. The patient died that night, and the bathroom was lost. And when the cadaver was rolled in for the postmortem, the pathologist, a crude type, turned to the nurse and said, "What the hell are these goddamn lumps on his belly?"

"Well," she said, "as long as he was allowed to have the borscht, I thought he might as well have a few boiled potatoes."

If *The Cherry Orchard* was my borscht, my boiled potatoes were of course the other and lesser comedies of Chekhov. Although they are all the works of a writer of genius, it is a steep dive from the grandeur of *The Cherry Orchard* to the provincial lassitudes of *Uncle Vanya*. But wherever you come to roost on these plays, you are still on very high ground in the theatre.

I had first thought seriously of *Vanya* when I ran into the late Paul Muni one day. Over a cup of coffee, I managed to keep myself awake while Muni subjected the play to an excruciatingly detailed analysis. Muni's analyses were legendary. Whatever they may have lacked in cogency, they more than made up for in thoroughness. When I was at last permitted to speak, I mentioned the possibility of his exchanging the roles of *Vanya* and *Dr. Astrov* every other week with Edward G. Robinson, a prospect which I hoped would appeal to an actor whose talent had been developed in repertory. I noticed that he had stiffened when I mentioned Robinson's name, and to my astonishment, he brought up the question of billing—whose name would be on top in the advertisements? Although neither Muni nor Robinson were then the stars they were to become in the films, I could foresee some very dreary possibilities in the situation. About stars I felt like the anonymous wit about women: it was more fun to make them than to keep them. And my interest in the project declined.

But the sight of Connolly's face revived it. Walter, I thought, would make a perfect *Vanya*. And Perkins, even without the romantic beauty and the distinguished style of Stanislavsky who created the part, might make an interesting thing of *Dr. Astrov*. The role of *Elena*, which seemed to me a rather old-fashioned portrait of a "teaser," I decided to modify, to suggest a beautiful and desirable women, chilled beyond hope of recovery by marriage to a withered windbag of a professor. (Miss Theresa Helburn of the Theatre Guild was offended by this very slight liberty but I assured her that dead authors were very tolerant; only innocent bystanders, always vulnerable, might be hurt.) And I asked Lillian Gish to play the part.

They say that there is nothing as dead as yesterday's newspaper. But perhaps they overlook things as remote as a theatrical production done more than forty years ago. During its entire lifetime in New York and on tour, *Uncle Vanya* was seen by some 200,000 people. According to actuaries, 85 percent of them are now dead and so, for that matter, is most of the cast. Although eternity has become, in Wellington's phrase, a damned near thing, what is called "human" is believed to be important and everlasting. And there was a good bit of the stuff in the making of *Uncle Vanya*. There were squabbles about money, though these were of a kind unlikely to be found in the theatre of today. There was even a moment when a member of my staff was convinced that Actors' Equity would not permit the play to open at all. And like an innocent maiden in one of the old melodramas, *Uncle Vanya* came very near meeting a fate worse than death from an elegant villain, lurking behind the scenes without so much as a pair of telltale mustachios.

The first of these problems made itself known one afternoon a few days before rehearsals were to begin. I heard what sounded like a howl of rage from one of the offices down the hall. I thought that Perkins, who had been waiting for his contract to be typed, was doing a little clowning with Hughie Schaff, my manager. Then my phone rang, and Schaff said, "Mr. Perkins refuses to sign his contract. As a matter of fact, he's just torn it up."

"Why?"

"If you don't mind, Mr. Harris, I'd rather let him tell you."

"All right, ask him to come in."

"You seem to have upset Hughie," I said to Perkins.

"Nonsense, he's just laughing himself to death."

"This business of tearing up contracts ... who the hell do you think you are—Toscanini?"

"I'll admit that was a touch of grand opera. But why the

devil was my contract made out for my full salary? You know perfectly well that Walter and I agreed to open on half-salary."

"Well, I never agreed to it."

"Look—we'd like to see this show have a little run. With the cast you've lined up and a flock of stagehands to pay, it will probably be too expensive to operate. And frankly, old man, Walter and I would rather get six weeks out of it at half-salary than three weeks at full salary."

"The answer is no. Everybody else in the company will be on full salary, so I can't have you and Connolly taking any cuts. Besides, if you take less than you are entitled to against a failure, you ought to get proportionately more than your regular salary if we have a success. And that would make you my partners. But I don't want any partners, so you'll just have to suffer along with the rest of the cast. Anyway, who knows? We may even have a hit."

"You don't really believe that?"

"Well, I don't believe in God, so I suppose I've got to believe in something. And I don't believe we'll have a flop either. Now go back and make your peace with Hughie and sign the bloody contract. Otherwise I'll be tempted to have you blackballed in every cotillion society in the country."

"By God, you know how to turn the knife, don't you? After a threat like that I can only bend the knee in submission." He sighed and shook his head. "Anyway, I did my best."

"If you'll excuse the expression, you and Walter are both noble fellows. Although I suppose that by the rules of the Actors' Equity Association, you are nothing but rats."

Being more philosophical by nature, Connolly made no fuss at all. "I firmly believe in letting everybody go broke in his own way," he said. "That's what democracy means to me."

But other trials lay in store for me. Toward the end of a night rehearsal a few days later, I noticed the tiny figure of Miss Kate Mayhew settled in the rear of the auditorium. Though her eyes were rheumy and her features worn, she was intently watching what was being done on the stage. Because of her age, I had rehearsed her scenes first, so her day's work had actually finished hours before.

"Why haven't you gone home, Miss Mayhew?" I said.

"Oh, don't worry yourself about me," she said. "I've been on stage since I was three, and I'm still stagestruck. I'm having a wonderful time."

According to the records, almost sacredly inaccurate in the theatre, she was then seventy-four years of age. And she seemed feeble when she was not on the stage. But there she was quick and alert and, almost from the first day, a delight in the part of the old family nurse. I had heard that she was looking after an old invalid sister. And I had discovered that, because the subway stairs were too much for her, she was traveling at least ten miles a day between 148th Street and Times Square by trolley car.

During a brief recess I walked over to a far corner of the stage where Eugene Powers sat, rolling a cigarette in brown paper, an act which he must have repeated fifty times a day.

"What a really marvelous play," he said.

"I hope you get at least a month in Barbados out of it." He looked frantically around for wood and finally tapped the leg of his chair. Born and bred in Maine, he lived for his holidays on that island. "Tell me something, Gene. Is Katie only seventy-four?"

His long horse teeth lent a false glint of malice to his smile.

"More!" he croaked, like a cut-rate raven. "More!"

That night I hired a cab to take Miss Mayhew home. She was infuriated.

"She raised so much hell you'd think she was being raped," said the stage manager after putting her in the taxi.

"What was the squawk?"

"Oh, the extravagance of the thing. She said she didn't like being babied."

"God, what a tight-fisted company."

"I honestly think she feels humiliated."

After that, a chauffeured car was engaged to take her home after night rehearsals. This service was continued on matinee days during the New York run.

One day I received the following letter:

To whom it may concern:
If you are courting me you are too young. If you are just playing with me, God will punish you (I think). Rid-

ing home in the trolley is not a hardship. It relaxes me and gives me a chance to catch up on all the gossip in the tabloids. So I feel much smarter than the folks lolling in their limousines. Now you have willfully deprived me of this small pleasure. Why I remain fond of you only Heaven knows.

Kate

To a Certain Party [I wrote in reply]

If I were courting you I would not descend to anything as underhanded as a few automobile rides. In matters of the heart I am inclined to be quite direct—even head-long, when the circumstances dictate. But now you have put a dangerous idea into my head. And the more I think of it, the more tempting it becomes. So perhaps it would be wise from now on to keep a small pistol in your purse, ready to defend all that a good woman holds dear.

T.W.I.M. Concern

Some of the best scenes around the theatre are never seen by the audience. Twice a week, on Wednesday and Saturday nights, Miss Mayhew could be observed emerging cautiously from the alley of the Cort Theatre. "She always kept hoping that car wouldn't be there waiting for her," said Eduardo Ciannelli, who played the saintly simpleton, Telyegin. "Then she would catch sight of the chauffeur holding the door open for her and stop dead in her tracks. She'd just stand there for a minute staring as if she couldn't believe her own eyes. Then she'd mutter, 'Oh shucks,' and climb in."

The kindest, most modest and self-effacing and, of course, the most beautiful member of the company was Miss Gish. Somewhat to my surprise, she was the greatest "problem" of all.

When I had phoned to ask her if she might be interested in playing *Elena*, she said, "I think I'd like to very much if I could see myself in the part." I offered to send a messenger around with a copy of the play. "Please don't trouble," she said. "I'll send my maid over to Brentano's and have the book here in half an hour." Before I left for home that evening, she called and said, "It's a lovely play. If you think I can do it, I'm willing to try."

A DANCE ON THE HIGH WIRE

The businesslike tone of this brief conversation, resembling nothing so much as a minor transaction between a grocer and a shopper, did not surprise me at all. I had met her several times with George Jean Nathan, to whom she was supposed to be engaged. There was absolutely nothing of the professional actress about her, let alone the great film star she had been. What struck me, even more than her rare, flowerlike beauty, was the impression she gave of an admirable and even formidable character. In her presence, it was Nathan who seemed, for all his worldly charm, a little actorish.

Yet she came to rehearsal in a palpable state of fright. As she had not been on the stage since early childhood, this was not altogether unnatural. "All these people in the company are so wonderful," she said mournfully after the first session. "I really don't think I'm good enough to be on the same stage with them." I laughed. "They're not all that wonderful," I said. And I told her that Helen Hayes was so nervous during the first week she rehearsed *Coquette* that she broke out in a painful rash. "And Helen," I added, "hasn't been off the stage since she learned to walk." If this was meant to reassure Miss Gish, it failed utterly. Her eyes clouded over with compassion, she murmured, "Oh that poor, poor girl."

Though adored by her fellow actors and constantly encouraged by me, Miss Gish only grew more despondent as rehearsals continued. There was never the slightest doubt in my mind that she would play her part beautifully, yet her self-confidence steadily declined. I felt mystified and impotent, like a physician watching the life of a seemingly healthy patient slowly ebbing away. My hope that she would last out rehearsals rested entirely on my confidence in her character.

"Can you hear her on stage?" I asked Connolly one day. Sitting in the auditorium, I had found her increasingly inaudible.

"Occasionally," he said. "It's the worst case of stage fright I've ever seen."

"What nobody here seems to realize is that Lillian is not just another actress. What she really is is an angel," said Perkins. "Mark my words—one day we'll see her rise from the stage and ascend toward the fly gallery. Then, like the Red

Sea parting for the Children of Israel, the roof will open, and she will be wafted back to Heaven."

"Yes," said Powers, "she is just too beautiful and too good for this damned planet."

From day to day there was no way of knowing whether Miss Gish would ever come to rehearsal again. And she was clearly entitled to stay away if she felt like doing so. She was not under contract.

I had thought of discussing the matter with George Jean Nathan. He had, in fact, telephoned me several times during the first week of rehearsal. But he did not ask me how Miss Gish was getting on. What he said was, "Do you think she can really play the part?" I was ungallant enough to wonder whether he felt concerned for her sake or for his own. Miss Gish was a rare prize among women. Would she still be a prize if she flopped as a stage actress in New York? In the end, I chose not to discuss Miss Gish with him.

My confidence in Miss Gish was not shared by Hughie Schaff. For five years, he had been employed as my accountant. His opinion of theatrical people was not favorable. He regarded them, one and all, as feckless and irrational. Yet he longed to be a company manager. Perhaps it was the story, all over again, of St. Paphnutius and Tháis, of the Reverend Davidson and Sadie Thompson. Now at last he *was* a company manager, and he was not happy. His thick, broad-bottomed, German figure had always plagued him with dietary problems. Now his clothes were beginning to billow around his frame.

First he was disappointed in my handling of the brief rebellion of Perkins and Connolly.

"This is a dollar-and-cents business. So why pay actors more than they ask for?" he said.

"That's a sensible question, Hughie," I said. "But I'm afraid it's really too late to do anything about it now."

Then, after watching a rehearsal, he was plainly disappointed in Chekhov.

"Do you think the public is going to pay good money to see these peculiar-type Russian characters?" he said.

"Your guess is as good as mine, Hughie."

A DANCE ON THE HIGH WIRE

But his greatest disappointment was reserved for Miss Gish. When he asked her about her salary, he was amazed to hear her say that she was too upset to discuss the matter. This in turn upset Hughie.

"Maybe it's just my inexperience," he said. "But have you ever heard of an actress making a remark like that?"

"Not that I can remember. But if she doesn't want to talk business, just leave her alone."

"Well, she'll have to talk about it sometime. Miss Gish has been in pictures all her life. Do you think she knows anything about stage salaries?"

"I really have no idea."

"Do you know what they were paying her in Hollywood?"

"Quite a lot, I imagine."

"She was getting $10,000 a week."

"Really?"

"Yes—really." He pursed his lips primly as if the figure were an obscenity. "Now, Mr. Harris, suppose Miss Gish asks for a salary along those lines. In a case like that, just what do we do?"

"I suppose we'll have to pay it. I don't see what else we can do."

"But what will happen to the show?"

"I guess we'll just have to close."

A shudder seemed to pass over Hughie. "As of this moment," he said after a slight pause, "you don't even know if she's going to open in the play. The way she sounded to me, I think there's a good chance she won't open. Have you lined up anybody to replace her in case she walks out?"

"No."

"But in case of an emergency, Mr. Harris, you must have somebody in mind."

"No. Not a soul, Hughie."

"Jesus Christ!" said Hughie, "I didn't have sense enough to know when I was really happy."

If what goes up must come down, it sometimes works the other way around. Out of a clear sky, late one afternoon Miss Gish said, "I wonder what the costumes are like. Do you think we might go over to Tappé's and have a look at them?"

All the accumulated tensions of the last ten days had vanished forever. The patient, so mysteriously ill, had mysteriously recovered. And since Miss Gish had never been given the slightest reason to suspect that there had been any tension, I asked no questions; I merely said, "All right, if you like." Triumphs have a way of escalating. Within the hour I would be savoring another one.

When we got into the cab, I noticed for the first time how dirty my hands were. So for that matter were my clothes. But Miss Gish, who had spent the day on the stage which was even filthier than the auditorium, was immaculate. I showed her my hands and said, "Beauty and the Beast."

Arriving at Tappé's on Fifty-seventh Street, we found all the salesgirls and manikins hanging on to the railing behind the shopwindow like birds on a telegraph wire, staring in awe as Miss Gish emerged from the cab. Perhaps something of her beauty had rubbed off on me; certainly there must have been something about me when we walked into the shop, something probably invisible to the uncorrupted eye. Bearing down on us with a broad welcoming smile, the distinguished dressmaker, Mr. Herman Patrick Tappé, extended both hands in greeting. The severe lines of his naval officer's jacket which barely contained his broad, obviously corseted figure, were brought into harmony with the prevailing atmosphere by an immense saffron-yellow silk handkerchief pouring in a cascade from his breast pocket. One can only suppose that he somehow failed to see Miss Gish. How else is it possible to explain that he walked past her, took both my hands in his, and said, "Girls, isn't he just too gorgeous?"

From that high point, the rest of this story is bound to go downhill. Miss Gish was enchanted with her costumes; the dress rehearsal was almost perfect, and the opening performance in New Haven was even better. There is usually a hectic period of rehearsal and rewriting following an out-of-town premiere. Here there was nothing but a spell of quiet bliss. Only Hughie Schaff remained grim.

"She's got us over a barrel now," he said.

"Who?"

"Miss Gish. She's sure sitting in the driver's seat."

"Just what the hell are you talking about, Hughie?"

"Don't you see? She's a hit now, and she's playing without a contract. So she's in a position to dictate her own terms—that's only human."

"Do you really believe Miss Gish is like that?"

"Oh, personally she's a lovely lady—no question about it. But where money is concerned, you've got to expect the worst in people."

"Has anyone ever told you you're a very cynical man?"

"No, I'm just practical. Don't you think I ought to talk to her now and try to settle this before things get out of hand?"

"No, wait till Saturday. Stop in her dressing room after you pay the rest of the company, and I'm sure you'll find her perfectly reasonable."

It irked Hughie to be denied a free hand where his business acumen was concerned. Being German, however, he did exactly as he was told. When he came back to the hotel after the matinee on Saturday afternoon, he was covered with sweat.

"They won't let you open in New York," he said.

"Who is they?"

"Equity. We have no contract with Miss Gish."

"You've spoken to her?"

"Yes, I've spoken to her." He was panting. "Believe it or not, she says she feels she ought to pay *you.*"

"Really? Did she mention a figure?"

"This is no joke, Mr. Harris. You're in a spot."

"Do you realize," I replied, "that it will be on every front page in New York if Equity keeps us from opening? That might be a big thing for a play with these peculiar-type Russian characters, and I think we ought to give it some consideration. Meanwhile, you'd better go back to Miss Gish. Explain the situation to her. I'm sure she's too good-hearted to force a whole company out of work in times like these. If she's too embarrassed to discuss her salary with you, just ask her to write a figure on a scrap of paper and, whatever it is, pay it."

The figure Miss Gish wrote on the corner of a bit of newspaper was just about what a good showgirl could command.

Hughie was elated and protested bitterly when it was very considerably increased. Like Hughie, Miss Gish also protested, and always believed that she had been wildly overpaid. Despite what Hughie regarded as my unforgivable extravagance, the entire investment in the production ($9,000) was paid off within ten days of the New York opening. The budget for the same production today would come to $175,000, and it is extremely doubtful that it would ever pay off. It is always agreeable to find something good to say about a person or period generally maligned. There were some very nice things about the Depression.

Sitting in a huge leather wing chair in the corner of the Taft Hotel lobby in New Haven after the performance on Friday night during our tryout, and swinging his beautifully shod little feet like a happy, idle schoolboy, was George Jean Nathan himself. He saluted me with his hands clasped high over his head. I waved and crossed the lobby to get the key to my room. I had already heard that he had been utterly delighted with the show. But I was not thinking of that. What I was thinking about was the kind of play the newspapers would have given the story if I had walked the other way and given Nathan a solid punch on the nose.

I had of course no intention of doing anything of the sort. Although whacking a dramatic critic is a recurrent fantasy among stage people, I have always regarded it as a gesture of pure farce, like shooting the president of the National Rifle Association with a mail-order pistol.

Besides, Nathan was a good friend and, more often than not, a delightful companion. He had an eye for a pretty girl and occasionally a tender glance for a plain one. And he carried his liquor like a gentleman. One evening as his guest at his favorite speakeasy on East Fifty-fourth Street, I saw him put away eight martinis. Then he looked at his watch and said, "I've got to cover a play tonight, so why don't we skip dinner and meet for supper?" I dropped him opposite the theatre. Through glazed eyes, I watched him thread his way through the tangle of traffic with the surefootedness of a sleepwalker. When he turned up for supper, he appeared to be as fresh and debonair as ever. "How was the show?" I said. "Perfectly horrible," he said cheerfully. "But thank the Lord, it gave me a wonderful appetite. Will you join me in one last martini?"

Now obviously you couldn't punch a man like that on the nose. Still, if I had done so, the papers would have had a field day. They would have described it as an unprovoked attack. And the Broadway columnists (where are they now?) would have worked themselves into a lather over the sheer perversity of the act, since I already knew how favorably disposed Nathan was toward my production. All would have agreed that it was a perfect example of my legendary unpredictability. The "facts," like perfectly trained servants, would have been at their command.

Unfortunately one small fact would have been missing. For by that time I knew for a certainty what I had only suspected: that it was Nathan who had robbed Miss Gish of her self-confidence. That it was he who had been trying to convince her that she was not good enough to play the part and to persuade her to quit the show. And it was he who had inflicted an incipient ulcer on Hughie Schaff.

By the time I got into bed, however, I had characteristically turned the matter over in my mind and come to a characteristic conclusion: that it was not Nathan, but I who was cutting an absurd figure. Suddenly I could see myself for what I really was—a small, inconsequential figure in a procession that stretches back to the beginning of time. Professional whores have always complained that their business was being ruined by amateurs.

❧ AN EPILOGUE OF SORTS: ❧
THE UNDERSIDE OF THE FAIRY TALE

NO DOUBT THE PRODUCTION OF *UNCLE VANYA* MAKES A pretty enough story. But in the year I had been away, the world had changed. And so had I. It seemed hard to believe that barely two years had passed since I stood on the brink of a really great adventure in the theatre—an adventure in which my fortune, even my future, would be at stake.

My experience with *Coquette* and *The Royal Family* had cured me of any lingering interest I might have had in the commercial theatre. Early on the morning after the opening of *The Royal Family* I was bundled up and deposited in a drawing room of a Palm Beach express train and remained in my berth until the train arrived in Florida. There I spent another three days in bed. I received a few calls from my office in New York. Apart from that, I spoke to no one but my room-service waiter. I slept a great deal and ate very little. But for the view of the sea outside my window, I might as well have been staying at the Belleview Hospital. Nevertheless I somehow managed to do a little thinking.

It now seemed clear to me that all the work I'd done on Broadway was merely an apprenticeship for what I hoped would be my real career in the theatre. The plays that I had produced were of course expertly devised entertainments. But they were not remotely in a class with the kind of plays I wanted to do. These I could not do because the necessary acting talent did not exist in this country.

I decided that I must either quit show business entirely or face the prospect of recruiting and developing a company of players and operate out of a theatre of my own. This would obviously be a very considerable undertaking. And while I could manage to furnish the capital for it, I would need a collaborator to share in the enormous labors that would be involved. But where was such a collaborator to be found? This problem occupied my mind for weeks. It was not until late March of 1928 that I telephoned Holbrook Blinn and asked him to have lunch with me.

Blinn, then almost twice my age, was not only a great star, but by far the most accomplished actor on the American stage. He was also a skillful director and producer. He had once leased a Broadway theatre and for a couple of seasons put on rather brilliant productions of first-class one-act plays. Most recently he had directed and starred in a charming trifle of Molnar's called *The Play's the Thing* and made it into a thoroughly delightful evening of theatre.

He was not only highly intelligent, but a man of character. The stinging rebuke he sent to the Baptist Church which had solicited him for a donation (the Baptists were then notoriously antitheatre, and they regarded acting as an immoral profession) received nationwide press coverage.

We sat down to lunch at twelve thirty at Voisin's Restaurant and did not rise from our chairs until almost five o'clock. I was delighted to discover that he knew the work of all the dramatists and the plays I discussed with him. Among many other matters we included Strindberg's *The Dance of Death*, Kleist's *The Prince of Hamburg*, Schnitzler's *Professor Bernhardi*, Hauptmann's *Hannele*, Pinero's excellent farce *The Magistrate*, the Quintero brothers' *Fortunato*, Feydeau's *A Flea in Her Ear*, Chekhov's *The Cherry Orchard*, and Molière's *Le Médecin Malgré Lui*.

"This is a red letter day in my life," said Blinn as we were shaking hands at the end of our first session. "I am absolutely with you in this thing. And I am so sure of its success that I'd be glad to put up some of the money to get it under way."

During the following weeks, our plans were developed to the point where we had agreed to spend a couple of months in England in the fall to recruit actors for our company.

I found an unexpected ally in William Randolph Hearst, who offered to acquire a plot of ground, a hundred feet wide, on Central Park South in the block between Seventh Avenue and Broadway that would extend into Fifty-eighth Street. I agreed to put up $300,000, and he would put up the land where I was going to build the kind of theatre I had long dreamed of—with rehearsal rooms, a scene painter's loft, a carpenter's shop, and comfortable office space for a very full staff that we would require. Mr. Hearst assured me that we would have no difficulty getting a bank to put up the rest of the money we would need to build the theatre. These brief weeks were the high-water mark of my passion for the theatre.

Then, only a few days before the first out-of-town performance of *The Front Page*, Blinn was killed in a fall from his horse. It was the first time in all my life I had been balked by death, and it hit me very hard. I suppose that the "little games" I was engaged in with Howard Hughes were a distraction from the unhappiest period of my life.

By the time I got back to Broadway in 1930, I had lost most of my fortune in the stock-market crash, Blinn was of course dead, and even Mr. Hearst was beginning to find it difficult to function as a baronial entrepreneur. Indeed, his vast collection of art and antiquities, which filled a dozen warehouses, had to be put on sale at Macy's Department Store to see him through his own financial difficulties. But even if Blinn were still alive and I still had all the money I had once possessed, and even if Mr. Hearst were still ready and willing to carry out the proposal to build a theatre, I don't believe I would have cared any longer to go through with it.

Coming into the theatre as an energetic and gifted amateur only five years before, I had managed to produce four great popular successes. In the seventeen years between 1930 and 1947, a period in which I was actively engaged in the theatre for ten seasons, I produced and directed only six productions that might be considered noteworthy: *Uncle Vanya, The Green Bay Tree, A Doll's House, Our Town, Dark Eyes*, and *The Heiress*.

But more often than not, during those seventeen years, I was also engaged in turning out a considerable number of flops. Where I had once been a tireless amateur, doing only those plays that had aroused my feelings, I was now nothing more than a bored professional, waiting like Mr. Micawber for something to turn up. The truth is, I had already had my little dance on the high wire. For me the theatre as an adventure was finished.

Being constitutionally prone to obsessions, I had replaced my obsession with the theatre for another one—one in which the stakes were not worldly success but actual survival. In Europe after the stock-market crash, I had found the time to take a long look at the world, and my prognosis was anything but hopeful. Among my friends were "Jimmy" James* and Walter Duranty of the *New York Times*, George Slocombe of the London *Herald*, and Arno Dosch-Fleurot of the New York *World*. Their private views of things to come were very different from the copy they sent to their editors. They furnished their newspapers the "news"; their beliefs and intuitions they kept out of their dispatches. These would soon leave me half paralyzed with apprehension. They were all dead certain that Hitler would come to power in Germany.

I had entertained few illusions about men and institutions. So I was not really shocked by the collapse of the stock market. In 1928, Harry Content, my stockbroker, phoned me in Florida one morning and asked if he might buy me 5,000 shares of English General Electric at the opening of the market. "I will sell them by two forty-five this afternoon," he said. By two thirty that afternoon the stock had jumped five points, and I was richer by $25,000 I did not need. The whole transaction depressed me. In a melancholy mood that night I convulsed my dinner companions by remarking that a world in which such coups were commonplace was bound to fall apart. Two of my guests would be suicides within the year.

What did shock me on my return to America was the moral

---

* Edwin L. James, then chief European correspondent and later managing editor of the *Times*. We had met in Paris as fellow crapshooters and became good friends. A tough ex-police reporter from Atlanta, who could talk to the most eminent politicians in France in the same bare-knuckled style he had employed with courthouse characters back in Georgia, he was a great favorite of Adolph Ochs and, at a slight remove, of mine.

and physical collapse of friends I had left, happy and confident of the future, less than a year before. I made futile efforts to save some of them. When I quit the theatre for the second time in 1940, I destroyed some $63,000 in promissory notes, all drawn by good honorable men who could not be expected ever to redeem them.

But the growing fears that possessed me had nothing to do with the horrors of the Depression. So once again, exactly as I had done as an undergraduate, I turned away to the world of books, this time almost exclusively to history, biography, and memoirs. To be sitting at White's Club in London, watching the great Whig leader, Charles James Fox, at the gaming table lose his entire fortune in a single night; or spending an evening in the somber dining hall in the San Souci Palace in Potsdam, as Frederick the Great in his frayed, badly spotted old military coat was sitting down to supper with his two aged Scottish marshals, all three of them swaying like dry reeds on the thin edge of senility; or to observe the Founding Fathers assembled in Philadelphia to prepare the Declaration of Independence, gorging themselves on six-hour-long dinners which left them just barely enough energy to write their wives of their exhausting labors in a noble cause—all these were far more real to me than the world I was living in.

Perhaps a long rambling letter I wrote in the autumn of 1938 to a friend in London will convey what my real feelings were like at the time. During the thirties I traveled a good deal. I crossed the Atlantic thirteen times in the decade before the war. Long afterward I realized that these "business" trips were merely a facade for my real purpose, which was to find brief interludes of relief in the womblike security of a stateroom aboard a transatlantic liner. Indeed traveling by steamer was one of the great pleasures of life. And when you could afford first-class accommodations, you could find respite from a world hell-bent for destruction.

If there was a single flaw among these pleasures, I suppose it was the tendency of people to walk the decks clockwise. Westbound aboard the *Normandie* one day, I chose to go the other way around. This was all very well—the only trouble was that you kept seeing the same faces over and over again.

One of these belonged to a lady whom the Victorians would have described as nobly proportioned. For myself, I would say she was a bit hefty, and leave it at that. But as her smile, each time we passed each other, grew unmistakably warmer, I thought it prudent to reverse my course. So I became once more part of the sheeplike promenade. Predictably, I soon found this irksome and turned off into the bar. To my astonishment the lady had somehow caught up with me.

"Do you mind if I ask you a personal question?" she said. Her voice was like overripe fruit.

"Certainly not," I said, entirely without candor.

"Are you by any chance Danish?"

I was sufficiently struck by this oblique counter to observe the lady more carefully. And I could not help calculating how much she might gain in elegance with the loss of a round dozen pounds. But that might well turn out to be a long-term project, and the *Normandie* was unfortunately a very fast ship.

"I'm sorry to have given such a misleading impression," I said. "I'm an American." And then, for some reason, I don't know quite why—possibly as an obscure defensive measure—I added, "And I'm a Jew."

It was as if I had declared myself an astronaut.

"How utterly fascinating!" she said. "I've often wondered what it feels like to be Jewish."

"It's really quite exhilarating," I said. "It's rather like performing on the high wire in tight shoes."

It was after this incident that I wrote the letter I have referred to:

Dear Michael,

I'm sorry my forebodings, as you called them, left you feeling so gloomy. Your great fault is that you are not merely English but so very goddam English. If you only lived on another island halfway around the world, I might urge you to join a political society and knock off a few of the dolts who are leading your country to ruin. In Japan political assassination is not so much a crime as a kind of respected civil right. I can see the horror in your eyes as you read these words. But after all, be a man—and what is better, an Englishman—and remember that you are descended from people who once beheaded a king—and what is far worse, they did it right after he had taken the trouble to have his beard beautifully trimmed.

It has been my chronic bad luck to get involved in arguments with Communists who have never read *Das Kapital* and with anti-fascists who've never taken the trouble to browse through the pages of *Mein Kampf*. They all know without reading it that it's psychotic. What they don't know is that it's a psychotic masterpiece. They think that because a book is full of absurdities, it can't be seriously intended. This may go down as the mistake of the century. And Hitler's ravings plainly reflect the fantasies of a large part of what is called Christian Civilization. If the Germans were really clever, they would get out an American edition of *Mein Kampf* and sell it for a quarter, or even give it away, like Gideon bibles. There are plenty of rich loonies in the U.S. who would be glad to contribute to such a worthy cause.

These "forebodings" of mine didn't seem to have quite so gloomy an effect on that very intelligent man, Vansittart. There is a style about that old boy which I suppose is fast disappearing from English life. But when I said I was afraid Hitler might slaughter the Jews in Germany, he smiled and said, "You have a highly theatrical imagination." It would appear that in matters outside my profession, a theatrical imagination is a disability, like epilepsy. Of course I did not mention Burke, Fox, Sheridan, Palmerston, or Disraeli.

What worries the hell out of me is that there is no one in Europe for the Jews to turn to. The Kremlin is run by a bloodthirsty son of a bitch who's murdered millions of Russians without turning a hair. He is hardly likely to trouble himself about the destruction of a few hundred thousand Jews. (Of course the Communists don't murder their people—they merely "liquidate" them—just as our mobsters "eliminate" them. Both debase a nobler tradition established a few centuries ago by the Roman Catho-

---

* We may take pardonable pride in our boys in Vietnam. They never liquidated, eliminated, or relaxed the natives. They did of course "waste" a few old women and children. But that, as we now know, was not murder either.

lic Church. Despite anything you may have read in the history books, the Spanish Inquisition didn't burn their heretics. They simply "relaxed" them.* Now it's of course easy to see that the stake was really nothing more than a Christian cure for nervous tension.)

A couple of years ago, I got to know a professional killer. He was a well-mannered, smartly turned out little fellow, something of a gourmet and to top it off, a real musical buff. We went to a couple of symphony concerts together, and I found him extremely good company. Of course we never discussed his professional life. And I'm sure he had no idea that I knew what he did for a living. One night, over a drink, I took my life in my hands and asked him point blank if his conscience ever bothered him about the people he had knocked off. My fears were wasted. "How can you be so silly?" he said. "They're nothing but lice."

Now poor Chink who as a matter of course got knocked off himself, seems as innocent as a child alongside of Stalin and Hitler. The really great killers are not these poor little gunmen, but the revolutionaries, the priests, the intellectuals, slaughtering for the good of humanity and the glory of God—fucking idealists all. Who was it— Blake?—who said, "Excess of sorrow laughs"? Well, there's nothing funnier on the New York stage than the antics of the seedy rabble that swears by Stalin to justify his crimes. Some of them are Jews. Probably the greatest fraud ever perpetrated against the Jews wasn't the Protocols of the Elders of Zion, but the rumor, disseminated by crafty gentiles, that they are clever.

By the way, I think I forgot to mention a most comforting *Boche* on the boat coming over. This bloke assured his table companions that the coming war will be "most humane." It seems that the Germans know down to the last centimetre of rubber hose just how much fire-fighting equipment you *Englander* have at your disposal. And it appears that their air force can *in one night* drop more firebombs on England and cause more fires than you have the equipment to handle. The result: England in flames and your government suing for peace. But the important thing to remember is that, while a regrettable amount of property will be damaged, very few lives will be lost. That is what makes the whole thing humane— see?

The most popular magazine in America* recently published an article by a General Motors official, full of admiration for life in Germany. In spite of what he called "some unfortunate excesses," he found the Germans happy and healthy, with jobs for everyone, while we in America are for some strange reason wallowing in a ghastly depression. The lesson for my countrymen was plain: "Despoil and humiliate the Jews, expropriate their property, drive them out of the professions and the universities, and then perhaps America too can be happy and prosperous."

There is actually very little concern in the U.S. for the condition of the Jews in Germany. Respectable people regard the crimes committed against them as "regrettable," while the boobs are inclined to enjoy the spectacle of the Jews "getting what's coming to them." And we are even under weekly attack from a cruddy Roman Catholic "radio priest" named Father Coughlin who doesn't refer to us as Jews but as "international bankers." It is the droll charm of his program that he pronounces both words with the elegance of a drunken stage-Irishman in high society. Heigh-ho.

In times like these when there are no "eternal verities" to cling to and no guide to the future except for the inexhaustible stupidity and malevolence of the human race, it is a little less than comic to find myself entangled in anything as trivial as the theatre. Especially now with the prospect of the most colossal production in history looming ahead of us. A show with a cast of millions, with giant settings high in the sky and in the depths of the sea, with the spectacle of shattered cities silhouetted against glorious towers of flame and corpses everywhere. How it will dwarf our most ingenious "stage effects." And we will owe it all to the stupidity of your politicians (and ours as well). Anyway, over the next few years, we are going to learn an awful lot of geography.

To quit the theatre, however, is more easily said than done. It's like trying to break off with a woman you no longer love but with whom you share enslaving memories. The worst of it is that the theatre is just about the only place in the world you are not asked your race, your religion, your antecedents. There are only two questions: Can you sing? Can you dance?

* *The Saturday Evening Post*

The real vice of the theatre is that it is a narcotic. Once you inhale the fumes, you forget who and what you really are. If history were only written by the great comedians of literature—by Voltaire or Heine, by Swift or even some untamed, bachelor Mark Twain—it might record that Herbert Hoover made more American communists than Marx, Lenin, and Stalin all put together. And that Hitler jolted me into the discovery that I am a Jew. A Jew, I may add with mixed feelings, who has just been taken for a Dane.

The widow of the friend to whom I had written this letter described it as "prophetic" when she very kindly returned it to me a few years ago. In the light of events, it is difficult to share her view. And I could now see that I had also been unfair.

It is altogether understandable that Lord Vansittart should have declined to share his political views with a mere New York theatrical producer. As the permanent under secretary of foreign affairs, he had held the highest office in the British bureaucracy. And his relations with me were entirely professional. We had met several times to discuss a play he had written about Melbourne. But the late Eugene Meyer, who after a brilliant banking career refurbished the Washington *Post* and helped make it probably the best newspaper in the country, also dismissed my fears at the time as "theatrical." However he was born a Jew, and I suppose I expected more of him. Like other distinguished men engaged in large affairs, he had obviously outgrown his origins.

Playing Cassandra is a tedious business and, after hearing another banker in San Francisco pronounce a German butchery of the Jews "absolutely unthinkable,"* I threw up the part. I might have gotten grim comfort from an entry in Virginia Woolf's diary, written on the day I spent in San Francisco: "A gritting day . . . *Capitulation will mean all Jews to be given up* . . . So to the garage." Her husband had set

---

* If experience has taught me anything at all, it is that in this world one must resolutely face the unthinkable and think hard.

aside some gasoline. If England fell, they would commit suicide together. The very least of the distinctions of Leonard Woolf is that he was a Jew. Being artists, not bankers, they understood what Hitler's victory over England would mean to the Jews. *And not only to the Jews in England.*

And I was tired of bankers. They had come a long way from the early days of the New Deal when, under investigation, the best of them might have been taken for imbeciles and the worst for common crooks.

In difficult times it is safer to turn for guidance to the poets. A hundred years before Hitler, Heine wrote: "Christianity has occasionally calmed the German love of war, but it cannot destroy that savage lust. Once the cross, that restraining talisman, is broken, the old Norse fury will take command. The old gods will arise from forgotten ruins and rub the dust of a thousand years from their eyes. Thor will leap to life and his hammer will bring down the cathedrals. When the crash comes, it will come like nothing ever heard in history. A drama will be performed which will make the French Revolution seem like a pretty idyll."

Heine's rich uncle Solomon in Hamburg took an extremely poor view of his nephew's prophesies. We must suppose that it is nothing more than coincidence that he too was a banker.

If politics makes strange bedfellows, history makes even stranger ones. Both gamblers, Pope Pius and I blundered into an affinity at the end of the war. He turned away from the world and fed his canaries. I, on the other hand, fed literally thousands of birds, to say nothing of a vixen and her two cubs during a hard winter in the country. I fed and became friends with countless deer. For a month one summer I entertained a family of raccoons, each properly seated around my garden table in a nightly supper of pears. I have enjoyed the trust of beavers, skunks, muskrats, and chipmunks. I have drawn whole clouds of migrating ducks and geese to prepared feeding grounds, and I can testify that amidst all their delirious chatter I never heard so much as a whisper about the blessings of Christian Civilization.

The defeat of Hitler's armies somehow fused Pius and myself into a bond of brotherhood. And so we both settled into a state of *decathexis*, a condition virtually incurable and therefore the equivalent of an annuity for a psychoanalyst.

(There are those who will regard this coupling of myself with the Pope as irreverent. But anyone who has seen Bishop Sheen, Norman Vincent Peale, and Billy Graham posturing on the television screen must be aware that organized religion, like politics, is now just another slum area of show business.)

The fact is that our intimacy, the Pope's and mine, began quite improbably, in the twenties when we were next-door neighbors at the Hotel Lotti in Paris. As Cardinal Pacelli, he was on a papal mission to the French government and we occasionally exchanged bows and smiles in the hotel elevator. What brought us even closer together was that he had, even more improbably, invited a good friend of mine to tea.

Georges Bram-Soroko, now a highly successful financier living in America, was then a recent law-school graduate, torn at the moment between two ambitions: a career as a banker and a place on the French Davis Cup team, no mean ambition in the days of Cochet, La Coste, and Borotra. A crack tennis player, he suddenly saw the possibility of gaining control of the Compagnie Generale Transatlantique, and with the help of a small group of friends he executed the coup, got the shares listed on the New York Stock Exchange, and acquired a great fortune before he was thirty.

But it was at the law school that he had first distinguished himself. His record was so brilliant that the dean urged him to study canon law. "You are likely to have a magnificent career in the law," he said, "and it will not hurt you to extend your studies in a field that may one day be useful. Besides, you may well find it amusing."

Very likely the dean had made the cardinal aware of Bram's exceptional gifts, for he now offered him a post with the Church.

"But surely, Father, you must know that I'm a Jew," said Bram.

"You needn't worry about that," said Pacelli, with his winning smile. "Come with us, and I am sure all will be well."

As he later recounted the incident to me, Bram had been very much taken with the worldliness and humor of the cardinal, who had discussed political matters with great wit. And the admiration was obviously mutual. In Rome on business in 1947, Bram was invited by the Pope to visit him at the Vatican.

"What was so remarkable about him was that he remembered everything we had discussed twenty-odd years ago," said Bram. "He even remembered the political predictions he had made and cheerfully admitted how wrong they were. 'But of course in those days,' he said, 'I was not yet infallible.' Naturally I laughed. But I knew that he had repeated that joke many times before."

Bram shook his head in commiseration. "The poor devil," he said. "Politics, not piety, was his real passion, and it destroyed him. And how could he be expected to intercede for the Jews in the death camps when Hitler was leading a great Christian crusade against the godless Russians? The Communists were the greatest menace that has ever threatened Catholicism. And they had fabricated a perfect parody of the Church with a world capital of their own, with a holy bible and a fanatical devotion to dogma, with an artfully preserved Saint Peter, and as if to etch this caricature in acid, a bearded Jewish Father."

But perhaps T. S. Eliot devised the perfect epitaph for the Pope:

> The broad-backed hippopotamus
> Rests on his belly in the mud.
> Although he seems so firm to us,
> He is merely flesh and blood.

With the "banal" tidings from the death camps after the war, I felt absolutely nothing. After fifteen years of private horror, I felt entitled to enjoy a benevolent numbness that could not be pierced by even the most appalling statistics ever recorded. So if the state of *decathexis* is a stroke of fortune for the most scoundrelly psychoanalyst, it is like a free suit of armor for the "victim."

So I can live with the spectacle of a President of the United States warning one of his daughters to stay away from museums lest she be contaminated by leftists and Jews—and smile. I can even smile at a general in charge of the national defense, earnestly warning an audience of college students that the press in the United States is entirely controlled by Jews. And I can even laugh at another President whose siblings are a professional faith healer and a boozy clown whose deepest political loyalties are devoted to the cause of Governor Wallace of Alabama.

But then, once in a great while, I am aware of a little crack in that armor. I see a picture of Willy Brandt standing with eyes moist in Jerusalem. Or read of young Germans spending their summers in the kibbutzim in Israel. And for a moment I recall the world of my childhood, when we believed in the Germany of Goethe and Schiller, of Heine and Lessing, of Beethoven and Bach, and of the days when we used to sing *"Die Lorelei"* in school and recite *"Du bist wie eine Blume"* and *"Dort wo die Citronen blühen."*

At such rare moments I go straight to my filing cabinet and extract a letter I received in 1968. It contained a bit of dialogue overheard by a friend of mine in a café in Vienna. An official of Euratom (the European atomic agency), my friend is not only a first-rate physicist but a master of shorthand. The speakers in the scene which follows were described as two middle-aged gentlemen, one of them wearing a tiny ribbon in his lapel:

1ST GENTLEMAN:	*Ja . . . if . . .* that is still the biggest word in our language.
2ND GENTLEMAN:	In all languages, Herr Kommandant.
1ST GENT.:	If Hitler had only been clever about the Jews . . .
2ND GENT.:	He was obsessed, poor fellow.
1ST GENT.:	Worse . . . he was stupid. Compared with the stakes we were playing for, all the confiscated Jewish capital put together was not worth a single night of English bombing.
2ND GENT.:	And how many of those nights we

	had to endure. My dear mother and two aunts . . .
1ST GENT.:	*Ja . . . ja*, that is all water over the dam. At least some of our best scientists were more intelligent. Privately they were very concerned when Fermi got away to America.
2ND GENT.:	I had no idea that Fermi was a . . .
1ST GENT.:	Fermi was not a Jew. He had a Jewish wife.
2ND GENT.:	Ah, so that was it. But that Meitner woman—wasn't she a Jew?
1ST GENT.:	Of course. Lise Meitner. One of our own people . . . an Austrian. They say she made a vital contribution. And even Oppenheimer, who managed the whole affair—did you know he got his training here with us in Germany?
2ND GENT.:	Think of it!
1ST GENT.:	There were all those damned Jewish brains involved in the whole thing. Einstein, Rabi, Slezard. Any price we paid for them would have been cheap as dirt.
2ND GENT.:	And they might have been working for us!
1ST GENT.:	*Ja . . . if . . .*
2ND GENT.:	It is nothing but sheer heartache to think of it, Kommandant. Now the one who made the hydrogen bomb . . .
1ST GENT.:	Teller—a Hungarian Jew—what else?
2ND GENT.:	Ach, it's pure torture.
1ST GENT.:	Even as late as '45 we could still have won it all. Even with our armies beaten. With our cities in ruins.
2ND GENT.:	We would have controlled the continent all the way to the Pacific.
1ST GENT.:	You talk like an idiot. We would have controlled all the continents. And no one could ever again hope to compete with us. Every physics and

	chemical laboratory in the world would have been under strict German control.... All scientific research—until the end of time.
2ND GENT.:	And here we are, paying blackmail to the Israeli ...
1ST GENT.:	And licking the asses of the damned French ...
2ND GENT.:	And when you look at the Russians today ...
1ST GENT.:	The Russians would have been the niggers of Europe. Two hundred million of them to do all the dirty work. We would have bred them like animals for every kind of unskilled menial labor.
2ND GENT.:	It would have been paradise.
1ST GENT.:	*Ja* ... paradise ...
	(They were silent for a moment, thoughtfully puffing on their cigars—of German manufacture, unfortunately.)
1ST GENT.:	... and that, my dear friend, would have been the time to settle with the Jews.

After I've read that bit of dialogue for perhaps the twentieth time, my customary balance is restored. I am once again stable, like the Austrian count who was asked how things were now in Vienna, the shrunken capital of a once glittering empire. "Hopeless," he said, "but of course not desperate."

❧ A BONUS ❧

I CONCLUDE WITH THE FOLLOWING SKETCH, ORIGINALLY printed more than ten years ago in *Playboy* Magazine and my first published memoir. It thus became the seed out of which this book grew, a debatable distinction, no doubt. What struck me in reading it over after such a long lapse of time was that I do not seem to have been as intolerant of show people as I had thought I was.

Pal Joe

One day in the thirties one of the editors of the Vanguard Press sent me a book with a brief note:

We are asking you as a great favor to read this novel, which we recently published. We consider it a brilliantly comic book but we have been unable to get any kind of sale for it. We would very much appreciate your opinion of it.

The book was called *Homage to Blenholt* and it was by an author I had never heard of—Daniel Fuchs.*

As I told the editor, the only reason I could imagine for the book's failure, over and above the normal idiocy of book reviewers, was its inept and utterly misleading title. How the devil was anyone to guess that *Homage to Blenholt* was a

---

* Mr. Fuchs is also the author of a delightful novel called *Summer People* and any number of superb sketches in *The New Yorker*. It is a pity that he has wasted so much of his life writing for the films.

novel about Jewish horseplayers and bookmakers in the Williamsburg section of Brooklyn?

The editor said it was the author's first book and that he was naturally very depressed. Would I be good enough to say a few words of encouragement to him?

The next afternoon Fuchs came to my office. With his dark, sorrowful eyes, he had the melancholy air of a failed rabbinical student. When I offered him a chair, he sat down and stared at the floor.

"I think I ought to tell you right off the bat that you have written a very funny book," I said. "And there is no question about it—you are a born writer."

Fuchs's eyebrows rose in bare acknowledgment. But he did not take his eyes off the floor. I wondered if the man was shy or whether, like the horse in the Mexican fable, he just didn't give a damn.

"What do you do for a living?" I said.

He seemed to reflect for a moment, as though he didn't quite remember.

"I'm a schoolteacher—substitute schoolteacher."

"I can't help wondering how anyone like you ever got to know all these bookmakers and small-time horseplayers."

"I just asked a cop on the corner where people go to bet on horses," he said, as though it was the most natural thing in the world to do. "And he took me over to a cigar store on the next block." I had never heard research described more graphically.

"You didn't by any chance become a bettor yourself, did you?"

Fuchs shrugged and nodded—regretfully, I thought.

"How have you been making out?"

"Well," he said gloomily, "I have been averaging about $150 a week."

"Really! You must have become a very good student of the form. Do you read the *Racing Form*, the *Morning Telegraph*?"

Fuchs shook his head. "I don't know how to read those things," he said. "I never bet unless I go to the track."

"You say you don't know the form. How do you pick the horses?"

I had to wait for Fuchs's answer. But when it came, it was starkly simple. And it was not the sort of answer to file and forget.

"My manager is something of a horseplayer," I said. "I hope you don't mind if I ask him to come in."

Joe Glick was a thick man with the thick, heavy, innocent features of a baby hippopotamus. He was almost painfully fastidious about his clothes. And, like all great dandies, he never changed his style of dress. Winter and summer, he wore dark, double-breasted suits and patent-leather shoes. And the gleaming surface of those shoes was matched by the high gloss on his quite perfect fingernails. To see Joe bent over his desk, his spectacles pushed over his forehead, delicately fingering the pinked swatches of fine English woolens his tailor periodically sent around to him, was to observe connoisseurship as though Rembrandt had painted it for the ages.

Naturally, Joe judged other people, first and foremost, by their clothes. It was therefore only logical that he should shrink from writers who, from Joe's observations, always dressed like bums. The only exceptions to this rule were Goodman Ace and Damon Runyon. But of course these fellows were not merely writers. They also happened to be dudes.

One of the great shocks of Joe's life was his first meeting with Thornton Wilder.

"You call that a professor?" he said. "I'll lay odds he's been wearing that suit for maybe twenty-five years. And I'll bet even money that he sleeps in it." At even money, I was of course compelled to decline the bet.

"Joe," I said, as I introduced him to Fuchs, "this young man is a very fine writer. He has just written a marvelously funny book."

"Is that so?" said Joe noncommittally. He had glanced briefly at the somber figure in the chair. Fuchs's suit was, at least in my opinion, in far better condition than Wilder's. But by Joe's exacting standards, the difference may have seemed superficial.

"I think you ought to know that you and Mr. Fuchs have something in common." If this was meant as a compliment, Joe was too polite to acknowledge it. "Mr. Fuchs is a horse-player."

Joe stared for a moment in Fuchs's direction and said, "I see."

"It may further interest you to know that Mr. Fuchs is a *successful* horseplayer. He's been winning on an average of $150 a week."

Joe's nostrils, which were large and almost barometrically sensitive, widened momentarily.

"That's a good average," he said impassively.

"But what I thought would be of particular interest to you, Joe, is the method by which Mr. Fuchs selects winning horses. For example, he doesn't read the *Racing Form.*"

"I see."

"Nor the *Morning Telegraph.* Nor the tip sheets."

"I see," said Joe, still in the even tone of a man patiently humoring a maniac.

"And he never bets unless he goes to the track and studies the horses for himself. And as they go by in the parade, he picks out the horses with the biggest breasts and bets them. Regardless of the form and regardless of the odds."

Joe took all this without flinching. He merely nodded his head very slowly, very deliberately. When at last he spoke, his voice was like velvet.

"Have you anything further to say to me Mr. Harris?" he asked with an unexpected show of formality.

"No, thank you, Joe."

The door was almost closed behind him when he pushed it back open again.

"Pardon me," he said. "Who, in your opinion, is going to win the big race next Saturday, Mr. Fuchs?"

Fuchs squirmed in his chair like a witness trying to avoid taking the Fifth Amendment. "As a rule I don't like to pick horses till I get to the track," he said, clearing his throat. "But in this case, I think I'm going to go with White Cockade."

Joe gave him a genuinely pitying smile.

"Do you realize," he said gently, "that this is a big stake race and that White Cockade is going off at about fifteen to one?"

Fuchs nodded sadly, like a man forced to acknowledge a bitterly damaging truth.

After Fuchs left, Joe came in and threw himself into a chair.

"Tell me something," he said. "Aren't you encentric enough on your own without bringing guys like this Fuchs around? How do you think he measures the size of the horses' tits anyway?"

"Exactly the way you and I do, Joe—by the finest of all instruments, the naked eye."

"It's lucky for him horses don't wear brassieres."

"A delicious idea, Joe. I wish I had thought of it."

"You do, huh? Can't you see what that would lead to? Only one thing," said Joe authoritatively. "Falsies."

A few days later I joined a friend for dinner at the Marguery. I had just sat down at the table when the waiter said I was wanted on the telephone. It was Joe.

"I have been calling every place in town," he said. He seemed out of breath.

"Why, has anything happened at the theatre? Anybody sick?"

"No, nothing like that," said Joe. "When can I see you? It's very important."

"I'll meet you at the theatre at ten o'clock," I said. "What's going on anyway?"

"I'm terribly upset," said Joe. "I'm going to stay drunk the whole weekend."

"Why not? It's a free country."

"That goddamn White Cockade won by five lengths. I tell you I'm sick."

"Well, Joe," I said, "I took the trouble to introduce you to an expert, and you laughed at him."

When I met Joe at a bar across the street from the theatre, he was in the act of tossing down a double Scotch. "Hit me again," he said to the bartender.

While the bartender was pouring the drink, Joe seized my hand. He was clearly overwrought. "Listen," he said, "I'm taking a living oath on my mother's life, do you hear? I will never bet a horse again as long as I live. I won't even read a form sheet.

"All right, Joe," I said, "but why let yourself get so upset?"

"Ah, I've been a sucker all my life," said Joe. "When I see a guy like this Fuchs, who doesn't know from nothing—" Here Joe broke off and gulped his second double Scotch. This seemed to steady him.

"Jed," he said, "you know what my mother means to me. She is the one and only woman I ever loved. You know I wouldn't break an oath, if I swore on my mother's life."

"I know, Joe."

"Now you know the type character I am. I'm swearing off now, and God knows I mean it, but maybe sometime in the future, maybe a year—maybe two years—from now, I'm liable to ask you to take me off my oath. Maybe I'll see a good spot for a bet. So I want you to promise me, as a pal, that no matter how much I beg, you will never let me off my oath."

Just how much Joe's mother meant to him I had discovered ten years earlier in Chicago. I had first laid eyes on Joe Glick on a damp October night in 1924 in the lobby of the old Pitt Theatre in Pittsburgh. I saw a heavy-featured, elderly man (Joe must have been all of fifty at the time). What he saw was a dark, skinny, savagely curt young man in a secondhand overcoat. Apart from anything else, my clothes were certainly not helpful. Obviously our meeting was mutually distasteful.

I had been sent to Pittsburgh to see a play called *Applesauce*, of which Joe was the company manager and part owner. Then, immediately after the performance, I was to take the night train to Chicago as advance agent for the show. The theme of the play, which I was of course duty bound to sit through, was that the best way to get along in life is to feed people applesauce. The author, otherwise undistinguished, had completely anticipated Dr. Carnegie.

Sitting out this harmless theatrical trash that night was like chewing on my own gall. For at that very moment I had expected to be the producer of *What Price Glory?*, which had just opened in New York and was to become the dramatic success of the generation. I had seen a good deal of Maxwell Anderson during the writing of that play, and he had promised me the manuscript. It had come as something of a shock to me that a man who could write in iambic pentameter could be so faithless.*

And now, reduced to nothing more than a mere advance man for a "turkey," I was walking rapidly out of a seedy theatre on a cold rainy night in Pittsburgh with this Broadway hustler, Joe Glick, tagging along after me as I ran for a taxi.

"What did you think of the show?" he said.

"Let me spare your feelings," I said. He was breathing hard. Even a little dash of a hundred feet seemed to have winded him.

"Don't you think it's a show for the public?" he asked hopefully. It was as though he and I might know better but then there was this huge, unperceptive thing, running into the millions, called the public. And it was this public that I was supposed to lure into LaSalle Theatre in Chicago.

"I don't know much about the public in Chicago. I've never been there before."

"You haven't?" It was like a cry of anguish. "You mean you

---

* On the day they were to deliver the finished manuscript of *What Price Glory?* to me, Laurence Stallings and Maxwell Anderson had breakfast with Alexander Woollcott, then the dramatic critic of the paper they worked for, the New York *World*. He urged them not to give the play to me for the simple reason that he had never heard of me. This damning evidence of my incapacity to do a play, coming from an "authority" like Woollcott, was enough to persuade them, without so much as a warning to me, to give the play to Arthur Hopkins. I had already borrowed the money to pay for the option on the play and had cast five of the smaller parts and the only girl in the play, a young Hungarian woman named Leyla Georgi. I sent them all to Hopkins' office, and every one of them was engaged for the parts I had cast them for.

In time Woollcott was to learn that I had a low opinion of him as a dramatic critic and that I laughed at his "style" as a writer with his addiction to a mannered vocabulary of tremolos, always touched with "rue" and "rosemary." I still have a letter of his asking me to promise not to read a piece he had written for the magazine *Good Housekeeping*, to which I replied with an equally short note: "I wouldn't read *Good Housekeeping*, even if you weren't in it."

I gave him a small interest in *The Front Page* to tide him over if he gave up reviewing plays. This brought him about $20,000. So, all in all, he did not come out too badly.

A DANCE ON THE HIGH WIRE

don't even know any of the newspaper people out there?"

"Nope. Not a soul."

"I wonder what in God's name Herndon ever sent you out for." Richard Herndon, a large man, almost never without a cigar, was the producer of the show and Joe's partner.

We were in the railway station, and the train was leaving in a matter of minutes. I handed Joe my train ticket.

"What's this for?" he said.

"I think you'd better get somebody you've got more confidence in," I said, "and I'll catch a train for New York."

"You mean you don't want to go to Chicago?"

"Not particularly. I haven't got much faith in your show. And if it doesn't go, you'll feel that it was my fault."

"But, my God, we're opening two weeks from Monday. Where am I going to get anybody on such short notice?"

I was walking rapidly to the ticket window to buy a ticket to New York when Joe grabbed me.

"Look," he said, "you go on to Chicago. I've got confidence you'll do a good job. I really mean it. Just try to get us a decent opening, and if we can stay in Chicago for two weeks without losing any money, I'll be your friend for life. I put every dime I got in the world in this show—so I must have confidence in you." It was with no confidence at all that I took back the train ticket.

By the time Joe and the company of *Applesauce* reached Chicago, after an unprofitable two weeks on the road, his mood was one of barely controlled desperation. He was now all but broke and so, I gathered, was Richard Herndon, the producer.

And Joe's dark, heavy features turned ashen when he discovered that I had committed him to the expenditure of almost two thousand dollars—which is what it cost to plaster the surrounding countryside with huge printed sheets advertising the show. This, of course, I had no right to do. I had also not been authorized to extend the show's contract for the theatre from two to four weeks, with options for the remainder of the season. But as business manager of the show, my signature was legally valid. And the obligations were ironbound.

Joe was in a state of panic. It now appeared that he had had no confidence in me from the beginning. That he was only trying to make the best of a bad situation. That he thought I looked like a tramp. That although he had been around for a long time he, like Alexander Woollcott, had never heard of me—nor had anyone else. All he could now see was a vision of bankruptcy, disgrace, and eventual suicide for himself. And when I laughed at him, we very nearly came to blows in the lobby of the theatre.

What had happened in the brief interval between my departure from Pittsburgh and the arrival of the company was that I had fallen in love with a brassy, broad-hipped, big-breasted dame with an Indian name. Chicago, I decided, was just jovial and tolerant enough to put up with the banalities of *Applesauce*.

The town was in its heyday. And I was given a welcome that would have brought tears to the eyes of a debutante at her coming-out party. In no time at all I had shaken hands with the cream of the elite—with Jim Colosimo, who was to become a historical footnote by introducing Al Capone into Chicago society, with Johnny Torrio and with Frank Nitti who was to become eminent as The Enforcer. These outstanding citizens I met under the sponsorship of Mr. Mike Fritzl, who operated an elegant speakeasy called the Friars' Inn. Mike, whose after-theatre guest I was to be almost every night of my stay in Chicago, became my social mentor. "Kid," he said, "I'm gonna learn you about life." And though he was innocent of iambic pentameter, Mike was not the kind to break *his* word. He even "learned" me a useful lesson in Christian theology.

"You hear bad things about people," said Mike one evening as a waiter brought me a fine china teacup filled almost to the brim with choice bourbon, "but you gotta learna use your own judgmen'." He waved a hand in the direction of Torrio, who was entertaining a party of friends in dinner dress at the far end of the room. "Look at them people over there—all perfick ladies and gennamen. Never tip my hat-check girl lessen fifty bucks. An' the waiter's always good for a couple hunnert." Mike drew on his Corona Perfecto and blew a fragrant cloud of smoke in my direction. "But now you take them goddamn religious conventions—they come up here from Texas and Oklahoma and all them places and I'm a son of a bitch if them crazy Baptists don't always wreck the joint."

Within a week I had a hundred friends on the newspapers. After the stuffy, stereotyped atmosphere of the New York press, Chicago was an absolute delight. It was a wide-open, utterly bohemian town, literally teeming with writers, artists, poets, and eccentrics, full of laughter and the best booze to be found in America. The editors gave me space in their sheets as if I were doing them a favor to take it. And I moved through the city rooms with the assurance of a professional freeloader and the nervous energy of a dervish. It was a town to which I was to help Ben Hecht and Charles MacArthur set up a kind of memorial in *The Front Page*.

At the end of the first week of the engagement, Joe looked like a man reprieved at the very last moment from a seat in the electric chair. The show had broken even. But the second week showed a profit of almost a thousand dollars and the third more than doubled that. The fourth week was just short of capacity, and thereafter the show sold out for months. And for the moment Joe was to be richer than he would ever be again until the day after his death.

An article now appeared in *Variety* bluntly attributing the success of the show to my publicity campaign. That evening, Johnny McManus, the saturnine manager of the LaSalle Theatre said, "Well, kid, a helluva lot of good this does you. You get the same lousy hundred and a quarter a week. So where's the percentage?"

Joe, who was present, looked embarrassed. The truth is that I had never even thought of this aspect of the matter. I had already decided to produce plays on my own, and I had no doubt that I would do so successfully. I was perfectly happy, but Joe, as it turned out, was not. As I was leaving the theatre, he said, "Listen—how come you've never made out an expense account?" He spoke like a man with a long-suppressed grievance. It was an event that he spoke at all, because we had never exchanged a single word since our row before the opening.

"Why should I?"

"Look," said Joe, "I know you've been entertaining all these newspaper guys. You can't knock around these speakeasies without spending money."

"I'd eat dirt before I'd make out an expense account for anybody like you to pass on."

Joe was so unsettled by this remark that he swallowed the insult. Upon recovering all he could say was: "After all you're entitled to get back anything you lay out for the show. That's only fair." It was a feeble counter, and I promptly knocked it down.

"Maybe you can get a court order."

The situation, unparalleled in the history of show business, might have given Joe a nervous breakdown. As if it were not bad enough to find himself under obligation to a mettlesome kid in obnoxious clothes, who had defied his authority, committed him to an outrageous gamble, and made the gamble pay off, he was now confronted by a sadist who refused to make out an expense account.

At the end of that week there was an additional twenty-five dollars in my pay envelope. As I felt that I had more than earned the increase, I made no acknowledgment of it. So things remained as they had been. But in Joe's eyes I detected an element of calculation.

I now discovered how a high-minded girl, after spending years shoring up every shred and morsel of her virginity, can lose it overnight. An expensive silk scarf arrived at my hotel with a card written in a familiar hand bearing the mysterious message: "From a Pal." Then there was a beribboned bottle of Scotch whisky "From your best Pal" and some neckties "For Auld Lang Syne." To McManus, constitutionally incapable of keeping a secret, I confided that I was being courted by a rich pansy.

The end was, I suppose, inevitable. I was in the office one night typing some stories for the Sunday papers when Joe came in. He looked hung over.

"I think I got a little out of line last night," he said. "And I guess I lost a hell of a girl."

It was like one of Hamlet's soliloquies, spoken into the empty air. I merely went on typing.

"Ah, the hell with it," he said. "There's always plenty more fish in the sea."

"Did you make that up?" I said.

"What?"

"That thing about more fish in the sea."

"It's just an expression. Didn't you ever hear it before?"

"No," I said. But my heart had softened, and I was lost. "You seem to want this fish back very badly."

"Well, she isn't the type you whistle for, and then she'll come running back," said Joe. "She's a very fine little lady."

I pulled the sheet out of the machine and inserted a fresh one.

"What's her name?" I said.

"Miss Taylor."

"Do you know her address?"

"Of course."

I typed rapidly for a few minutes and handed him the sheet. "Sign this," I said, "and ring for a messenger."

"Am I supposed to sign it without reading it?" said Joe.

"I thought you wanted to get Miss Taylor back. Now it seems you want to catch up with your reading."

Joe stared doubtfully at the letter. "I don't think she'll understand this," he said. "What's this word?" He pointed a polished finger nail.

"Lucubrations."

"Okay, if you say so. But what does it mean?"

"It means you were standing around, scratching your behind and wondering what to do."

"Gee, that's certainly a high-class way of saying it." Joe signed the letter and went backstage to talk to Walter Connolly, a member of the company. I had a date for the evening and left shortly afterward. On my way to Henrici's restaurant, I stopped briefly in a florist's shop.

I got back to my hotel at one and found two messages from Joe, asking me to be sure and call him at the Club Rendezvous. When I got to my room, the telephone was ringing. It was of course Joe. He was with Miss Taylor, as happy as a child, and asked me to come over and join them.

"The whole thing worked beautiful," he said. "How much did the flowers set you back?"

"Put it on my expense account."

At the end of the week I found that Joe *had* made up an expense account for me. Everything was carefully if inaccurately itemized, and it came to exactly seventy-three dollars and ten cents. Though I took the money, I must have seemed too distant in manner. This cost me almost twenty-four dollars. My expense account for the following week, neatly typed and signed "JBG, Mgr.," came to only forty-nine dollars and fifty cents.

The next night Joe insisted on taking me out. In the Balloon Room of the Congress Hotel Joe's status was noticeably high. And he brought his own Scotch whisky, which was very fine.

"Stick with me," said Joe, "and you'll get the best."

After a few drinks Joe took out his wallet and carefully extracted a faded snapshot of himself. Underneath the coarse features, inside the double-breasted suit that gave bland lines to the heavy figure, there had once been a nice-looking youngster who had sung and danced for a few seasons in the musical shows in the old Casino Theatre in New York. He had even turned actor for a while—a fact which he confessed with some shame. (Joe did not like actors. Like myself, he had a passion for performers.) But as if to mitigate this fault, Joe explained that he had confined himself to character parts. "Anyway," he said, "I never had the figger for anything else."

For a season he had toured in a show called *Under Southern Skies*, playing the part of an old Negro servant. Indeed, he performed so well that he got a few engagements to play *Uncle Tom* in stock. To my astonishment he recited almost the whole part in an accent which was not at all stage-Negro. It was the real thing. As he went on, his voice gained in depth and resonance, and when he came to Uncle Tom's dying speech, he did it with a pathos so genuine that it could not possibly have failed to affect an audience in the theatre.

"I had them sobbing so loud when I did that speech that I never heard a word of it," said Joe. And I have no doubt that he was telling the absolute truth.

But Joe set little store by his triumphs as an actor. What occupied the most sacred place in his memory was his season as company manager for the Dolly Sisters. (Perhaps it should be explained that fifty years ago, the bewitching Dolly Sisters, Rozika and Jancsi, were, unlike the Gabors of today, talented singsong girls and *real* international stars.)

"Ah, those were the days," said Joe. "A hundred and fifty one-night stands in a season. I'm prob'ly one of the few guys left who can lay out a route from Walla Walla, Washington, to Augusta, Georgia. And I can do it right this minute out of my head. And what good is it? All the friends I had in those towns—the theatre managers, the transfer people, the railroad men, the hotelkeepers—they're all prob'ly dead by now. And so is the show business I knew." I wondered how old Joe really was. "But what a time I had with the Dollys. We had a private car all to ourselves—just for the three of us—and it was specially decorated and furnished for the girls. We had maybe twenty cases of champagne stacked up in one end of the car and all the kosher salami you could ever hope to eat. The Dollies were Hungarian like myself. And how they could put away that salami. Now my stomach is too delicate for that stuff but in those days I was a pretty good *fresser*. We had a little party every night after the show, and we never got to bed before three or four in the morning. And how we laughed. My God, what a book I could write if I only had your vocabulary."

That was the night Joe and I got to be "pals."

We were approaching the end of our run in Chicago when Joe summoned me early one morning to his princely quarters at the Congress Hotel. It was barely eight o'clock, and I was surprised to hear from him at that hour. "Please get over as fast as you can. The maid will let you in."

This sounded ominous, and I dressed quickly. I discovered Joe in bed in pale-blue silk pajamas. When he saw me, he broke down and wept.

"What's the matter, Joe?" I said. "Shall I get a doctor?"

"I've already seen a doctor," said Joe. "I don't need any doctors. I want you to do me a great favor. I'm going to be out of action for a while, and I want you to handle both ends of the show for me. Will you do it?"

"Certainly." I thought Joe had found out he had cancer.

"But for Christ's sake, I think you ought to tell me what the hell is the matter."

"I'll tell you what's the matter. I've got the clap."

I could hardly stop laughing. "I've known a lot of people who got the clap, but I've never seen anybody take it so hard. Are you in pain?"

"It's not the pain," said Joe bitterly, "it's the goddamn humiliation. I've been knocking around all these years, and this never happened to me before."

"At least half of the people I've known in show business have had the clap. It's more like a professional courtesy. Do you know who gave it to you?"

"I wish I did," said Joe. "I would break her ass for her. The whole thing is I've been snoshing around with too many people." He blew a long, sombre blast into his handkerchief. "Show business isn't what it used to be," he said sorrowfully. "Do you know something? I've got a little money now, but I'd give every dime I've got in the world just to be back once more with the Dolly Sisters." He carefully dried his eyes. "I think I'll go home to Cleveland."

"When?"

"Today. I'm going to have my mother take care of me."

"Really? Will your mother know what to do?"

"Don't worry about my mother," said Joe. "My mother knows everything."

And he did go home to his mother, something it is difficult to imagine anyone else doing in similar circumstances excepting perhaps Johann Wolfgang Goethe and Sigmund Freud.

Ten years had gone by, and Joe was now employed as my general manager. At any rate, not even the most cynical reader can any longer doubt Joe's feeling for his mother. Joe had taken his oath on a Saturday night, and it is only fair to acknowledge that he remained absolutely true to it until quite late the following Thursday afternoon. Even then there was no actual breach, but with the aid of a radioscope a very fine fissure might have been detected. He brought a copy of the *World Telegram* into my office and jabbed a finger in the lower left-hand corner of the front page. "Look at the price of the winner of the second race," he said.

Although I have forgotten the name of the filly, I can still remember the price—$66.40.

"I have been following that hoor for a whole year. I know the people who own her. The least I would have had on her today was a twenty-dollar bill." He whipped out a little pocket notebook and peered down his bifocals. "At this moment," said Joe, "she owes me exactly $350, so I would have been even and a little ahead."

"It's too bad, Joe," I said, I'm sorry to hear it."

"Well," said Joe philosophically, "I've made my bed, and I guess I've got to lay on it."

"If you lay," I said, "it may be fun."

"*Oser*," he said. "With my luck it would probaby be pure agony."

On the following day a friend invited Joe to the track. Like an obedient child, he came to me for guidance.

"Do you think I should go, Jed?" he asked innocently.

"Why not? Except that I understand it isn't much pleasure when you're not betting."

"I was thinking the same thing," said Joe thoughtfully.

Joe was obviously waiting for me to say something more, but I seemed to be absorbed in a manuscript I had been reading.

"Jed, would you consider doing me a great favor? There are two horses running this afternoon that I know like I know my own name. I might be able to make a fantastic parlay."

"Well, I don't see how I can, Joe," I said. "In the light of your oath."

"That's what I mean," said Joe. "Would you, as a special favor, let me off my oath?"

"I'm sorry, Joe," I said, "but you know I can't do that. You remember I promised you, as a pal, that I would never let you off."

"Well, you know I was upset at the time."

I undertook to look severe. "Are you going to run out on your oath?"

"Oh, no," said Joe.

"Are you going to claim that you made it at a time when you were drunk, or not in your right mind, or under duress?"

"Oh, no! No! No! Of course, I wouldn't do anything like that. But you saw how upset I was."

"How many times have you told me you were a lifetime loser? Didn't you say you figured you had blown about $150,000 on the horses?"

"I admit it," said Joe miserably. "I don't deny it."

"Do you want to go back and buck guys like Fuchs who can make a living at the track out of sheer ignorance of form?"

"Every time I think of it, I want to shoot myself." Joe gave a deep groan. "You're absolutely right," he said. He stood there for a moment, a soul in torment. "You really think I shouldn't go, huh?"

"Well, you know the temptation, Joe," I said, "and you know what your mother means to you."

Joe nodded sadly and went back to his office. That was at ten thirty. About three quarters of an hour later he came back in his topcoat. "I think I'll go down to the track after all," he said mildly.

I said "Okay. I hope you will have as good a time as you can under the circumstances."

"Jed," said Joe, "would you reconsider?"

"What?"

"Letting me off my oath . . . You know damn well if I should make a bet today and anything happened to my mother—well, I don't have to tell you that that would just be the end of me."

"I know, Joe."

"And how will you feel about that? You'll feel bad too."

"Not as bad as you will."

"Jed, as a pal . . ."

"Wasn't I your pal the other night?"

"Jed, I'm begging you. Please take me off the hook."

I gave a fair, but I think only a fair, performance of being judicious. What I suppose I should have liked to do at that moment was to get up and put an arm around Joe. And that was the only moment I remembered, as I looked at him, not quite ten years afterward, lying in his coffin at the Riverside Memorial Chapel, during an otherwise entertaining funeral.

"All right, Joe," I said, "I'm taking you off your oath. But remember—I'm doing this only for the sake of your mother." It was Joe who threw his arms around me and kissed me.

From that time on I had a certain power over Joe. After all, I had very possibly saved his mother's life.

Joe almost always found words, like winners at the racetrack, in short supply. And he often called upon me to furnish missing parts of sentences. One of his dearest friends was a lawyer with whom he enjoyed ribbing matches late in the afternoon over the telephone. When I came into the office one day, I found Joe already on the phone. He quickly put his hand over the mouthpiece. "Tell me something I can call Munroe."

"Don't call him anything. Just ask him when he last committed barratry with a girl."

"Wait a minute," said Joe, "is that all right to say over the telephone?"

"The telephone happens to be in my name," I said. "And don't pretend to be so innocent about barratry. I'm sure you have done it a hundred times."

"Never!" said Joe, raising his right hand. "I'm one hundred percent normal. The natural way is good enough for me."

Joe lowered his voice. "When is the last time you committed barratry with a woman?" he said into the telephone, and then looked up at me triumphantly. "Munroe is hysterical," he whispered. I could hear his friend screaming with laughter, and then I heard Joe's voice: "Don't worry about me. I know all about barratry and not from experience the way you do."

If Joe had a single passion, it was that of a collector. Not of coins or of matchbox covers, not of silver tankards or Meissenware or tropical butterflies. Joe collected doctors.

Like most bachelors of a certain age, Joe treasured all sorts of ailments, most of them of a very obscure nature indeed. He was thus a natural target for all sorts of quackery, and it was only natural that he should be addicted to diets of one kind or another. For weeks at a time he would have an early dinner of hay, vinegar, and chopped nuts at a health-food restaurant on Forty-eighth Street. Afterward, he sometimes joined me at Moore's or Frankie & Johnny's where I might be enjoying a steak or a slice of rare roast beef.

"How can you put that stuff into your system?" Joe said one evening. "Do you realize what you're doing? You're eating dead animals."

"The animals I eat," I said, "are all dead circus animals. So after all, I feel I'm eating old friends. I'm what you call anthropophagous, Joe."

"I'm not surprised," said Joe. "It prob'ly comes from committing so much barratry."

I was puzzled but nevertheless impressed by Joe's loyalty to his diet. It was not like him to deny himself any of the pleasures of life for the sake of mere good health. But one day his friend and fellow manager, Benny Stein, gave away the secret of Joe's iron self-discipline.

"Right this minute, Joe's got a whole Stage Delicatessen salami stashed away in the closet of his room in the St. Moritz," said Benny. "And do you know what the son of a gun does after he finishes his oats at the health-food joint? He hustles up to his hotel in a taxi and puts away a good six inches of salami. I caught him at it one night. Then he brushes his teeth, gargles his mouthwash, and comes to the theatre with an expression like Mahatma Gandhi." Needless to say, I never betrayed Benny's confidence.

Like an exotic herb in a dish of plain cooking, there was a streak of cunning in Joe worthy of a vizier—a discovery I was to make after a late-night phone call. The bell woke me out of a drugged sleep.

"I hate like hell to wake you," began Joe.

"What's the bad news?"

"It's damned bad. Dale is quitting the show."

"You're kidding."

"No. He just phoned me."

"How can he quit? He's under a run-of-the-play contract."

"I reminded him that he'll prob'ly never be able to work

A DANCE ON THE HIGH WIRE

again. But he says he's prepared to take the consequences. It's supposed to be some kind of a personal problem. I'm getting dressed. I'm going over to his hotel to talk to him."

"What time is it?"

"One forty. Well, you can't say I didn't warn you."

James Dale was an English actor then rehearsing an important part in *The Green Bay Tree**, which was to open in ten days. He was not exactly ideal for the part. In search of the "right" actor, I had made fruitless journeys to London and Hollywood. And in finally settling on Dale, I was merely repeating the experience of a friend of mine, a decorator, who had spent long days haunting the best shops on Madison Avenue for a few yards of antique yellow Chinese silk, only to end up in Gimbel's basement with a bit of goods that was neither antique nor yellow nor Chinese nor, for that matter, was it even silk. However painful it may be to be stuck with a lousy actor, to find him suddenly indispensable is something fit only for the palate of a *Feinschmecker* in the field of humiliation. Since I had spent the last two days fighting a losing battle with the flu, my own palate was in no condition to savor the occasion.

And Joe *had* "warned" me. He was to join me for dinner after Dale, freshly arrived from London, came to the office to sign his contract. I was having drinks with Gregory Ratoff when Joe turned up a little late and still reeling from his first encounter with the actor.

"I had quite a job getting him out of the office," said Joe. "He just couldn't stop talking. And you might as well know, he doesn't think much of your casting ability. He thought it was very odd of you to cast him for a gentleman. A gentleman's gentleman seems to be more in his line."

"He is damned well right."

"What the hell is a gentleman's gentleman anyway?"

"A gentleman's gentleman, Joe, is a valet. And a gentleman's gentleman's gentleman holds the gentleman's gentleman's gear while the gentleman's gentleman brushes the

---

* Of this production, Brooks Atkinson of *The New York Times* wrote: "Mr. Harris has delivered a thunderbolt. You feel that the theatre has emptied itself of all its resources. It is difficult to believe there will be anything left for tomorrow." And it marked the emergence of Laurence Olivier as a great dramatic actor.

pants of the gentleman. Anyway, in London everybody considers him quite mad."

"Mad or not," said Joe, "in my opinion the son of a bitch is crazy."

"My fr-rand, dot is awnly par-rtly tr-rue," said Ratoff, who was at the moment absorbed in an artistic problem of his own. With nothing but a thin square of toast, a butter knife, and a little dish of chopped chicken livers, he had succeeded in molding an almost perfect miniature of the Great Pyramid of Egypt. "Dees weel keel me," he muttered, as he raised it to his lips, "I guar-ranty you." Ratoff's English often leaped and shimmered like a hooked game fish, and it occasionally soared to a peak of accuracy unknown to mere scientists and scholars. So I waited patiently as he chewed this immense morsel in a state of bliss in which there was no hint of mortality. "Joe," he continued, "I geeve you de lawdown on dees fallow. I worked in a peecture weeth him in London. He is not awnly cr-razy, but he is also one hundred procent insane."

I was just beginning to doze off when my telephone rang again. It was a little after three in the morning.

"Well," said Joe, "not to prolong the suspense, Dale is bound and determined to quit the show."

"You said it was something personal. Is he sore at anyone?"

"Oh, no. He says you've been wonderful to him. Now hold on to your hat. The personal thing is that his sister in London is about to have a baby, and he feels it would be a terrible thing if he wasn't there right by her side."

"Joe, are you implying that he's been screwing his own sister?"

"I thought the matter was too delicate to go into."

"Ah, you've made the whole thing up. I'll bet he never had a sister."

"And for a parlay, you can bet he never had a father either. Anyway, I promised to book him out on the first steamer we can get him on. And I got him to write us a letter giving his reason for resigning from the cast."

"Except for the honor of framing it, what good is it?"

"You never know. Meanwhile I'm wiring all the other people in the show that the flu will keep you in bed for twenty-four hours. So there's nothing else for you to do but shut off your phone and stay in bed and leave everything to me. In your condition you can't do anything else anyway. So why not make the best of it?"

I now took a large dose of sleeping tablets and slept for fourteen hours. Joe was just coming into my apartment when I woke up. He had poured himself a glass of Scotch, and he looked very tired when he sat down alongside my bed.

"You look a hell of a lot better than when I last saw you," he said. "I booked Dale out on the *Carmania* sailing tomorrow night."

"That's splendid, Joe. As of tomorrow, we have neither a show nor anything like a respectable balance in the bank. But I must say that it's a comfort to find myself associated with a first-class travel agent."

"I also took the liberty of offering him the services of your secretary to help him with any shopping he might want to do for his poor sister. Y'know, that almost broke him down. Still and all, he seems to be bothered about one tiny little thing. He somehow got it into his head that you'd answer his letter very graciously and accept his resignation—you know, like one of those letters Sir Herbert Beerbohm Tree would write to Sir Henry Irving."

"Sometimes your ignorance is a little unnerving, Joe. Tree was Irving's competition, not his manager. By the way, you don't think you might have inadvertently said anything to Dale to suggest that I might write him such a letter?"

"Of course not. How could you think such a thing?" said Joe, his eyes fixed firmly on a small bird enjoying a snack on my window sill. "I only said you wouldn't file a formal complaint against him with Equity. Just because I said you were sympathetic is no reason for him to expect you to consent to a breach of contract." I watched Joe carefully but, like the Almighty Himself, Joe watched the sparrow. "After all," he added, "that would be unnatural."

There was a slight, tentative tinkle on my office connection.

"That's for me," said Joe. "I told the girl to phone me here if Dale called." He took the phone and said, "Okay, put him on. . . . Well, old boy, how are you? Have you finished packing yet? . . . Oh, you've been thinking things over. . . . I see. . . . Well, I must say, this will be a big surprise to Mr. Harris. . . . I don't know. . . . I haven't had a chance to talk to him yet. . . . For all I know he might have other plans by now. . . . By the way, which side of the boat do you like to travel on? . . . Oh, I see. . . . Well, after I speak to Mr. Harris, I'll get in touch with you. . . . Not at all. . . . Good-bye." I took the phone from Joe and hung up. "Well, the limey's flat on his ass. It seems we've been so wonderful to him that he can't bear to desert us."

"What a hell of a time to be forgetting his sister—after knocking her up. As a retired actor what do you think he did all this for?"

"He just wanted to play a little bit of theatre. He thought there was going to be big emotional scenes. He expected us to plead with him—maybe even offer him a better contract. When he got nothing but sympathy and cooperation, he didn't know which way to turn."

"And then there was the letter, of course."

"Yeah . . . I think I'll let him stew in his own juice for a while and then call him after dinner. What time will rehearsal be tomorrow?"

But when a curious situation arose in connection with the booking of *A Doll's House*, Joe was not quite that subtle. Arrangements had been made for a long preliminary tour of this production prior to its New York opening. And these arrangements were quite perfect except for one thing—we could not seem to be able to get into Milwaukee. No matter how much we juggled the schedule, it seemed impossible to find a date for an engagement in that town, which was sure to give us a profitable week. Day after day Joe went to the booking office and returned with the same story: "They just can't get us in there." (This was a little ironical because Mrs. Fiske is said to have given the very first American performance of *A Doll's House* in Milwaukee—in the back room of a saloon.)

One night I invited Joe to have a drink with me at Frankie & Johnny's. And I had asked Johnny to put the very best bottle of Scotch in the house on my table. Joe was favorably impressed with the whisky. "This is something you shouldn't drink," he said. "It should be sipped."

He was well into his third glass when I said, "What have you got against Milwaukee, Joe?"

"What do you mean—what have I got against Milwaukee? What kind of a question is that?"

"It's a good question, and it expresses exactly what I mean. I haven't been around show business as long as you have, but still I've been around. And I've never heard of a situation like this. So the thought struck me that perhaps you don't like going to Milwaukee."

"If I don't mind going to dumps like Toronto and Buffalo, why should I mind going to Milwaukee?"

"That's what I'm trying to find out."

"Do you know something? You should see a doctor."

"I have consulted a very good doctor, and he said, 'Your Joe's got some inhibition about going to Milwaukee. Why don't you get him to see a doctor?'"

"Well, your doctor is crazy, too. I've got sore feet from walking back and forth to the booking office. Why would I do that if I didn't want to go there?"

"Your inhibition is supposed to be in your unconscious. It's there all right, but you're unaware of it."

"You can tell your goddamn doctor I haven't got an unconscious. Maybe he's got an unconscious, but I haven't got one."

As the Plimsoll line in the bottle sank lower and lower, Joe sank with it into a state of utter relaxation. Like a little boat that has slipped its mooring and drifted this way and that with every ripple of the tide, his talk shifted from further reminiscences of his beloved Dollys to a glorious tour of duty as general manager for the Shuberts in Kansas City. There the dames, according to Joe, were the best in the world. I was growing a bit drowsy when I heard Joe say, "My God, just sitting here and talking about dames," he said slowly, "I thought of something that was prob'ly the worst tragedy of my life. And you won't believe this, but I had completely forgotten it." He fell silent. In answer to my unspoken question he shook his head and said, "No, I can't tell you about it because you'd only use it against me."

"If I'm the pal I'm supposed to be, why would I do anything like that, Joe?"

"Because of one thing. It happened in Milwaukee."

"A tragedy, Joe, in Milwaukee?"

"Yeah. A hell of a tragedy. It's a wonder I ever lived through it. It's funny how the subject of Milwaukee came up tonight, and I never even thought of it."

"Maybe you have got an unconscious, after all, Joe."

"I suppose after you've had the clap, you're bound to get everything else. It was years ago—way back during Prohibition. I was handling a big musical show for Charlie Dillingham, and we packed them in for eight solid weeks in the old Garrick in Chicago. On the night we closed, the snow began to fall, and the stagehands and the transfer men had to work like hell to get the show into the baggage car before it began to turn into a blizzard." Here Joe paused again.

"You were going to open the next night in Milwaukee?"

"Yeh-ow," said Joe, as though I had helped him over a hurdle, "that's right. Well, when I got into the train in the morning, the club car was full of vaudeville actors. They were all on the bill that was going to open the next day in Milwaukee. And two of my best pals, Nate Leipsic, the coin manipulator, and Walter Kelly were on the train. It turned out to be a long ride on account of the snow drifts. But I'd brought along a good bottle of Scotch, and we had a drink all around. And what with one thing an another, I got to telling them about a marvelous gal I had been with in Chicago. This dame was so crazy about me that she'd written ahead to her best friend in Milwaukee—a Mrs. King—to look out for me when I got there. So I was all fixed up for the week in Milwaukee, and I guess I couldn't help bragging a little about it. Anyway, by the time we got into Milwaukee, we were three hours late. There was no problem about the business because we had been sold out a week in advance. So once we got the show into the theatre we were in the clear.

"I shaved and showered before going over to the theatre. I was just going out of my room when my phone rang. It was Mrs. King calling to welcome me to Milwaukee. I invited her to the show, but she said she was practically snowed in, and maybe she would try the following night. And she said she was so glad that her husband had gotten away the night before. He was a traveling salesman, and his itinerary had

A DANCE ON THE HIGH WIRE

been all set. The thing was that I had never heard a more wonderful voice in my life. There's only one word to describe it—it was beautiful. And the more she talked, the more I felt I just had to see her. So I asked if it would be all right if I came over later that evening. Well, it seems she was absolutely crazy to see me, but she lived a way out, and she was worried that I might not be able to get transportation in that weather. I told her to just leave everything to me, and I would bring along some good Scotch, and she said that would be lovely. I took the address, and I was in quite a state when I got to the theatre. Everything was fine backstage and in the box office. Of course the phones were ringing with people trying to put their reservations off until later in the week, but naturally we couldn't accommodate them because all the seats were gone.

"Well, the curtain was up, and everything was shipshape. So I went into a delicatessen next door and wound up with a big paper bag with about thirty-five dollars worth of *nosherei*, and the treasurer of the theatre got me two bottles of Scotch from the best bootlegger in Milwaukee. So now I had these two big paper bags loaded to the top and the only hard part was to get a taxi. The number was a way out on the north side of town, and no taxi driver would go out that far. It took me about an hour to get a guy to take me, and he wanted fifteen bucks. Well, I had gone this far so I just had to go through with it."

Joe filled his glass and took a good swig at it.

"It was a ride I'll never forget. We skidded and slid up and down whole mountains of ice. Every rut in the road was frozen, and I was more than half frozen myself by the time we got out there. The cab couldn't get anywhere near the curb. There was no curb—the snow must have been three, four feet deep. And all I had on was a pair of rubbers. But the worst thing was there wasn't a single light showing in the house. Luckily I told the guy to wait a minute and left the bags in the cab. I waded in snow up to my ass and climbed the front steps of the house and rang the bell. Nothing happened. It was like a nightmare. My legs were soaking wet from the snow. I started back to the cab. The driver was still trying to maneuver the car around, and he was cursing like a son of a bitch. Well, to make a long story short, I had to pay the bastard another fifteen bucks to get me back to the hotel.

"My hands were so cold by the time we got to the hotel that I couldn't even take my wallet out to pay the guy. The doorman had to do it for me. So I came into the lobby with those goddamn paper bags in my arms. And all those lousy vaudeville actors were sitting around. One of the guys said, 'What have you got there in those bags, Joe—anything good to eat?' So a bellboy carried them upstairs for me and opened the door to my room. When I saw myself in the mirror, I almost fainted. There were little white blotches all over my face and on the tip of my nose. I tell you, I was a wreck. I turned the cold water on in the washbasin and actually screamed like a lunatic when I put my hands in. It was like putting your hands in boiling water. For a minute I thought I was going to break down and cry like a baby. Thank God I had a little Scotch in my room, and I took a good shot. Then I kept on letting the cold water run and put my hands under the tap for maybe a second at a time. It hurt like hell, but little by little the circulation began to come back, and at last I was able to take off my wet pants.

"Just then the telephone rang. It was Mrs. King. She said, 'Oh, Mr. Glick, I've been conscience-stricken all evening about letting you come tonight. I'm so glad I caught you at your hotel before you could get away.' I said, 'What are you talking about? I rang your doorbell almost an hour ago, and a man stuck his head out of the window and the house was pitch dark.' 'But, Mr. Glick, there is no man in this house since my husband went away last night. And all the lights in my house are on. Where did you go?' So I gave her the address she gave me. 'Oh, my God, Mr. Glick, how could you have done such a thing? You went north, and I said south—don't you remember? I can't begin to tell you how terrible this makes me feel.' I thought she was really going to start crying. I could tell she really meant it. And then there was that beautiful voice. And I could see myself in the mirror over the dressing table, and the splotches on my face had cleared up."

Joe tossed the rest of his drink and shook his head.

"This is the hardest part of the story to tell. I know what I'm going to tell you is absolutely true, but I can't believe it

A DANCE ON THE HIGH WIRE

myself—do you know what I mean? It sounds like a goddamn lie, but it's the truth. I said, 'Okay, I'll be there as fast as a taxi will take me.' "

"Oh, no!" I said.

"Oh, yes," said Joe relentlessly, "that's the way it was, and I'm giving it to you straight. I changed my clothes, and I looked fine, if I do say so myself. Those actors were still in the lobby when I got downstairs. And they ribbed me a little bit. They wanted to know where I was going with those packages, and I said, 'Don't you wish you knew?' Then of course I had a little trouble getting a cab but nothing like the first time. This guy only held me up for ten bucks, and I felt pretty good when I got into the cab—you know, like when you're getting a bargain. Even the road didn't seem so bad as it was the first time. That shows how you can get used to practically anything. If I had a decent voice, I think I would have sung a little bit just to pass the time.

"By the time we got to the two thousand numbers, there just weren't any more houses, and her number was twenty-four hundred and something. The driver said he was willing to take me as far as I wanted to go but there was nothing like a house the rest of the way—it was all just undeveloped scrub with nothing on it. By this time I finally got it into my head that something was very wrong. So I told the driver to turn around and get me back to the hotel.

"And it seemed to turn ice cold when we started back, and pretty soon I was shaking like a guy with palsy. By the time I got back to the hotel, I was half dead. The doorman carried the bags in for me. And I stood in front of those actors in the lobby and cursed them for a solid ten minutes. I called them everything in the book, but all they did was laugh at me. And maybe a half dozen of them got into the elevator with me and helped carry the stuff into my room."

"Just what happened, Joe? Who did this to you?"

"A female impersonator named Schari with the most beautiful soprano voice you ever heard. I spent the whole week in bed with a terrible cold. And I never got to see Mrs. King at all."

"What happened to all that wonderful delicatessen?"

"Those goddamn actors ate it all."

Late in the afternoon of the following day, Joe walked into my office and announced that as a result of a cancellation, Milwaukee had become available for our schedule of *A Doll's House*.

"It's a miracle," he said. "Don't you think so?"

"Well," I said, "it has certain elements of a miracle. But naturally, Joe, one can't help being aware that in some ways it's rather a coincidence."

Joe shook his head. "I know what you're thinking," he said. "But you're wrong. Believe me, you're wrong."

"Okay, Joe. So be it. After all, what's a miracle or two between friends?"

There comes a moment when the kissing stops, and the best of miracles are at long last at an end. And so Joseph Blaine Glick found himself, on his last day on earth, on a raised platform above the pulpit of the Riverside Memorial Chapel, in an impressive coffin where he lay, exposed to the chest, in his dinner jacket, his solid features the color of wood violets. Indeed he looked as if he had been made up by a drunken barber or by a staff cosmetician trained in high-fashion interior decoration.

Joe had died at three o'clock of the previous morning after an almost perfect day. He had won a good bet at the track, and he had consumed the choicest part of what he sometimes called a "dead animal" for dinner. And from all I could gather, he had finished up the evening with a handsome Scandinavian friend, his Swede, as he called her, although he occasionally referred to her as "the Finn." In addition to this, according to the assistant hotel manager, a not quite completely consumed portion of salami was found on Joe's night table.

As Joe's two closest friends, Mike Todd and I were the chief pallbearers. The occasion was the fulfillment of an ambition Mike had for us to be partners in a production. It was shortly after I had produced a comedy called *Dark Eyes*. Mike, as I gathered from Joe, was something of a plunger at the racetrack. I knew that Joe, who was managing Mike's production of *Star and Garter*, was taking huge advances from the theatre-ticket brokers to cover Mike's losses.

"I never know from time to time," said Joe "whether I will be able to pay my bills. But every once in a while, Mike will come breezing in with twenty or thirty grand in cash and say, 'Joe, stick half of this away in the vault, will you?'"

"Do you share a vault with Mike?"

"Well, not exactly," said Joe somewhat mysteriously.

Now Mike and I were collaborating on our first and last production, and without false modesty I can say it was a great success. The place was packed, and everybody in show business seemed to have turned up. And as I stood there in the formal attitude of a chief pallbearer on one side of the chapel, with Mike in a beautifully cut black cashmere suit on the other side, I could only regret that Joe could not see the immense crowd that had come to do him honor.

After the eulogies, which were painfully dull, I was glad to see Rabbi Bernstein of the Actors' Synagogue mount the platform. Having had little experience of funerals, I hoped the rabbi might shun these banalities and say something real, perhaps something even droll and tender about Joe. But he only did what I suppose he was paid to do, and lit into the Twenty-third Psalm like a firehorse.

Now the air of the Memorial Chapel was suddenly rent by a low, moaning cry, "Joe! Oh, Joe!" It came from a blonde in the second row on the right. This must be the Swede, I thought, and not by any means bad looking. Then, hardly more than a few seconds later, the voice of another blonde, a few rows back on the left, floated into the air with all the authority of a prima coloratura. "Joe!" she cried. "My darling Joe!"

There was a stir among the mourners as the blonde in the second row rose to stare in the direction of the blonde in the sixth row.

As Rabbi Bernstein was saying, "He liddeth me beside the steel wawder," the two ladies exchanged a brief, chilling glance, that glance which is the secret nightmare of every gentleman who has ever played both ends against the middle.

Unfortunately, at this moment, Todd's eyes rolled in my direction. A great tidal wave of laughter rose all the way up from my guts, hammering violently at my throat. I was terrified. If I ever began to laugh now, the funeral would become a shambles. In desperation I clamped my teeth over my lower lip and held on grimly. As Rabbi Bernstein finished the psalm, a streak of blood was running down my chin.

But at last the business was over, and Mike and I were in the street making our way into a bar.

"You didn't know that the Finn and the Swede were two different dames?" said Mike.

"No," I said. "And I pray that Joe forgives me for having considered him too ignorant to know the difference."

"Well, this is one time he won't have to square himself," said Mike. And then we both began to laugh. But Mike, I thought, laughed longer and harder than I did.

"You're really hysterical, Mike," I said. "Why don't you swallow your shot and pull yourself together?"

Mike wiped his eyes with a handkerchief. "How much do you think Joe's estate is going to amount to?"

"I have no idea."

"I thought you would know," said Mike. "You were the one person in the world he was really close to."

"I assume he was in good shape," I said. "He even offered to stake me when I came to town to do *Dark Eyes*."

"Well," said Mike, "whatever he had, the minute he conked out he was $25,000 richer than he was before." Mike began to laugh again. "Joe had twenty-five grand of mine in cash in his vault, and for good reasons I can't claim a penny of it. Isn't that beautiful?" he said.

So on his last day on earth, Joe won a good bet at the track, enjoyed a choice of blondes, and had his last supper of salami. And then, to top it off, he deftly and effortlessly picked up a bonus of $25,000. Surely there are worse ways to leave this world.

How old was Joe? Nobody seemed to know Joe's age. When I was young, he seemed old. But as I grew older, he did not seem old at all.